Trackless Wastes
&
Stars to Steer By

CHRISTIAN IDENTITY IN A HOMELESS AGE

Trackless Wastes & Stars to Steer By

Michael A. King

HERALD PRESS
Scottdale, Pennsylvania
Waterloo, Ontario

Library of Congress Cataloging-in-Publication Data
King, Michael A., 1954-
　Trackless wastes and stars to steer by : Christian identity in a homeless age / Michael A. King.
　　p. cm.
　Includes bibliographical references.
　ISBN 0-8361-3513-X (alk. paper)
　　1. Identification (Religion) 2. Authority (Religion) 3. Bible—Evidences, authority, etc. 4. Sociology, Christian. 5. Church and the world. 6. King, Michael A., 1954- . I. Title.
BV 4509.5.K48 1990
270.8'29—dc20　　　　　　　　　　　　　　　　　　89-26865
　　　　　　　　　　　　　　　　　　　　　　　　　　　CIP

The paper used in this publication meets the minimum requirements of American National Standard for Information Sciences—Permanence of Paper for Printed Library Materials, ANSI Z39.48-1984.

Scripture designated RSV is from the *Revised Standard Version of the Bible,* copyright 1946, 1952, 1971 by the Division of Christian Education of the National Council of the Church of Christ in the USA. Used by permission.

TRACKLESS WASTES AND STARS TO STEER BY
Copyright © 1990 by Herald Press, Scottdale, Pa. 15683
　Published simultaneously in Canada by Herald Press,
　　Waterloo, Ont. N2L 6H7. All rights reserved.
Library of Congress Catalog Card Number: 89-26865
International Standard Book Number: 0-8361-3513-X
Printed in the United States of America
Design by Paula M. Johnson
Cover art by Gwen Stamm

1 2 3 4 5 6 7 8 9 10 96 95 94 93 92 91 90

*To the memory of
Elmer and Lillian Detweiler
and Cora and Irvin King,
my grandparents.
They inherited and passed down to me
that warm blanket and fierce tiger
which is my faith.*

Contents

Foreword by William H. Willimon 11
Preface and Acknowledgments 13

Introduction 17

CHAPTER 1: Our Homeless Age 24
   The Homeless Age 25
      The Homeless Age and the Mennonite Experience
      Secularization
      Modern Transportation and Communication
      Plurality and Pluralism
      Relativism
      Individualism
      Loss of Authority
   Two Attempts to Find a Home 35
      Separatism
      Translationism
   Questions for Discussion and Reflection 43

CHAPTER 2: The Bible and Tradition:
                 Three Approaches 44
   A Clash of Paradigms 46
      Precritical Understandings of the Bible
      Precritical Understandings of Tradition
      Critical Understandings of the Bible
      Critical Understandings of Tradition
   Marrying Critic and Precritic 57
      Direct Inspiration Mediated Through Humans
      Timeless Historicism
      Semi-Open Universe
      Simple Complexity

    Rational Piety
    Flexible Authority
    Making the Marriage Work:
        The Essential Role of Community
    Questions for Discussion and Reflection 65

CHAPTER 3: Taking the World into the Bible 67
    Plausibility Structures and Individual
        Perspectives 68
    Taking the World into the Bible: The Theory 71
    Taking the World into the Bible: The Building
        Blocks 73
        Biblical Orientation
        Biblically Oriented Community
    Results of Taking the World into the Bible 83
        Reversal
        A Community of Outcasts
        Biblical Politics
    Questions for Discussion and Reflection 87

CHAPTER 4: Connecting Bible and World 89
    Building a Critical and Self-Conscious
        Foundation 89
    Building Translationist Bridges Between
        Bible and World 93
        Systemic Thinking in Sociology and
            Family Systems Theory
        Bridging Bible and Experiential-Expressivism
    Psychology as Source of Enlivening Perspectives.. 97
        Four Ills/Four Antidotes
        The Limits of Psychology
        Using Psychology to Recapture Biblical Truth
    Questions for Discussion and Reflection 113

CHAPTER 5: Joining Separatism and Translationism: The Centered Congregation 115
   Models of Congregational Structure:
      Three Options 116
      Separatism: Rigid Boundaries
      Translationism: Few Boundaries
      Separatism and Translationism Joined:
         The Centered Model
   Implications of the Centered Model 122
      Conversion
      Church Membership
      Gentle Authority
      Strengthening the Center
      Homosexuality: A Case Study
      Limits of the Centered Model
   Questions for Discussion and Reflection 136

CHAPTER 6: One Way and Many Ways 137
   Intrafaith Interaction: Three Options 137
      The Bounded Model
      The Unbounded Model
      The Centered/Contextual Model:
         One Center, Many Expressions
   Interfaith Interaction: Three Options 145
      The Bounded Model
      The Unbounded Model
      The Centered Model
   Questions for Discussion and Reflection 157

**Epilogue: Trackless Wastes, Stars to Steer by,
      and a Home for Homesick Souls** 158
   Questions for Discussion and Reflection 166

Notes 167
Bibliography 172
The Author 179

Foreword

When I was sent the manuscript of Michael King's book, I wondered if someone had made a mistake. After all, I'm a Methodist, not a Mennonite. Mainline, liberal, Methodist, bless-almost-anything ecclesiology is supposed to be about as far removed from the separationist, exclusivist, sectarian Mennonites as is Durham from Des Moines. What could a Mennonite, struggling to embrace his church family, say to a Methodist, trying to embrace mine?

Plenty, that's what. Sometimes, the only way home is through someone else's yard.

G. K. Chesterton once said that there are two ways to get home. One way is to leave home and then to return. Another way to get home is never to have left. I believe that Michael King writes for those of us who have taken the first way home. His own faith journey began as a child in a Mennonite missionary family. Growing up within what he calls a separatist church, King experienced that church as a community of believers who were clearly set apart from the world. From there, in his young-adult years, King ventured into the "modern world." Losing patience with what he felt to be the narrowness, the exclusiveness, the biblical literalism of his church, he embraced the pluralism, relativism, and critical character of the world outside the Mennonites. He attempted to make his faith "relevant" to the demands of a brave new world.

Eventually, this pilgrim into modernity discovered that the modern world was a troubled, muddled place. In leaning over to speak the language of the world,

Christians had fallen in. With the help of the new critics of modernity as well as his own experiences as a pastor, King explored the realm of the post-modern Christian. He caught a vision of a church which neither nailed its doors shut to the world (deeply troubled though still sought by Christ) nor kicked open its doors to the world (all too willing to co-opt the gospel for its own selfish pursuits). In short, he returned home with a fresh appreciation of the church which first told him the story, with new insights for living that story in today's world.

Out of trackless wastes, Michael King leads us forth, wisely steering a course set by stars which do not deceive. If you have given up on the church because it is too critically closed or too uncritically open, if you have lost your direction on that perilous path called discipleship, if your house of faith is beginning to crumble, or else you haven't even yet begun to build that house, read this book.

I began to read *Trackless Wastes and Stars to Steer By* while I was on a cross-country speaking tour, pondering its pages in a succession of forgettable motel rooms far from my home. How well it described our predicament as modern believers. How clearly it named our situation. How simply and straightforwardly it charted an exciting new path for contemporary disciples.

I finished this book on a cold January night in Nebraska. Full of fresh insights, I put it aside and stepped out of my room into the cold, dark night. I was still far from home, yet the stars shone bright and clear.

—William H. Willimon
Dean, Duke University Chapel
Durham, North Carolina

Preface and Acknowledgments

In that wondrous piece of autobiographical theologizing called *The Alphabet of Grace*, Frederick Buechner says that "most theology . . . is essentially autobiography." I agree, which is why in this book I often make explicit connections between my personal story and my theology.

Given that stress on autobiography, I want to credit some of the people who speak through me, in their many and varied and sometimes contradictory ways.

First comes my aunt Evelyn King Mumaw. I think this book began the day she handed me the blanket. It was heavy and warm. One side was plain. On the other side, surrounded by red roses, roared a fierce tiger.

Aunt Evie told me my grandfather and his dates kept warm in their buggy under the blanket. Later it kept my dad and his siblings cozy. That blanket came to symbolize for me both the warmth of my inherited home of faith and its fierce demands.

When Aunt Evie gave it to me, I was groping back toward the tradition it represented but still feeling ambivalent about it. I preferred the grace, freedom, and joy I was finding through immersion in various psychologies.

But the blanket tugged at my soul and drew tears. It stirred me to love what it stood for. I resolved to be true to my blanket and simultaneously true to the wisdom I was finding among people who knew nothing of my blanket's world. This book is the result. I wrote it for myself and all who yearn for warmth in a chilly world.

Next come two people without whom I wouldn't exist, much less write: Aaron and Betty King, my parents. They'll probably wince (as I imagine they always do) when they read one more published critique of ways I experienced my background as constricting. As any good child should, I have a few bones to pick. But only a few, these days, probably far fewer than my daughters will have if they ever (God forbid!) theologize about *their* background.

After wincing, I hope my mom and dad can hear what I'm most deeply trying to say—that the family home they (and my eight sisters and brothers) gave me made an excellent model for building a theological home.

When I tell of the day she walked my agnostic self around the college library for three hours, explaining why she saw not only random molecules but God in falling autumn leaves and sun setting sweet on Massanutten Mountain, she'll know who she is: Joan Kenerson King.

Our friends thought it couldn't work—I so faithless, she so faithful. But it did, as we wrestled with each other's beliefs, as God entered the wrestling, as together we built a faith blending the best of both our ways. We share life, love, our children. We also negotiate who does what when. She gave me time to write this; I owe her, I know. I also owe Kristy, Katie, and Rachael, who knew the writing was done when they got their dad back.

Then come uncles and aunts, too many on my dad's side to be named (though I sneaked Aunt Evie in), but important, nevertheless. They remind me there's power and beauty in a commitment to God so deep that giving up radios and TV's and other "worldly" things is seen as small sacrifice.

On my mom's side are two uncles. Probably without knowing it, Robert Detweiler, intrepid adventurer and explorer, taught me to delight in roaming to the far corners of my soul. Richard C. Detweiler, wise and gentle church leader, taught me that my soul was God's and helped me see the church as a good home base from which to explore.

My professors at Eastern Mennonite College deserve mention. The late Anna Frey took a shy, scared college freshman under her gentle care. She listened to my doubts and hopes. She also sensed how much I wanted to write and taught me most of the few rules of English I remember.

Willard Swartley showed me that critical thinking and faith can go together. Titus Bender came to EMC too late to teach me in the classroom, but I got to know him and Ann anyway, and learned, by watching how they live, to love the parts of myself and others that are hurt, torn, outcast.

I met other mentors at Eastern Baptist Theological Seminary. Vincent and Charlotte DeGregoris taught me to let God's voice speak through stories, feelings, dreams, and visions. Peter and Carol Schreck stirred me to make peace with my family and church backgrounds and showed me the gold hidden in them. They helped me see myself as a "stodgy liberal," someone who could only be healthy by holding "conservative" and "liberal" influences in creative tension, rather than opting for either. We argued about it, but Ron Sider finally convinced me the universe is open to God's action. And he got me started on book writing by inviting me to coauthor a book with him.

Germantown Mennonite Church offered a vital laboratory for developing and testing my ideas. Though the views expressed herein are indeed my own, Germantown was to them what soil is to seeds. Because I couldn't stop, I won't start naming those countless Germantown people I came to love. But I can thank them for tolerating my novice pastoring, for pushing and challenging and supporting me, for offering precious glimpses of how to build a Christian home in a homeless age.

James C. Longacre, trusted adviser and crisis manager, oversaw my work at Germantown. He gave me space to try out my wild ideas and helped me clean up the mess when they didn't work.

Daniel Hertzler and David E. Hostetler published my articles often enough to make me believe in myself and rejected them often enough to keep me humble.

Loren Johns was my trusty editor at Herald Press. Putting it through computer analysis to bolster his case, he gently and correctly prodded me to simplify and polish my first draft. Then he skillfully polished some more. After Loren left Herald Press, S. David Garber faithfully saw the project to completion.

I thank them all, as well as friends and influences beyond number, scattered across the world and roaming through my being.

Introduction

> We seem . . . to be suspended in what the anthropologists call a liminal time, a time between the fading of the old stories to live by and the emergence of new ones. A character in one of John Updike's novels refers to it as "one of those dark ages that visits mankind, between millennia, between the death and rebirth of gods, when there is nothing to steer by but sex and stoicism and the stars" (*Couples,* 372). Surely we can do better than that. Our believing communities must work to fashion stories we can share and live by.¹

We're in a liminal time, says Robert Detweiler. *Liminal,* the dictionary says, has to do with what relates to or is situated at the limen. *Limen* means "threshold."

The hope of our time is that we stand at the threshold of a new age. Ours is the frightening but also spine-tingling task of sailing across the ocean to find the new world somewhere ahead, not too far now beyond the horizon.

The sadness of our time is that we're lost, wandering lonely across a trackless waste, searching the sky for stars to steer by. Though we catch a twinkle of stars in those rare nights when the smog of our time rolls back, they don't yet offer guidance. That's because no one has ever gone quite this way before. Until the stars are charted, they tease and haunt us with their promise of a guidance they can't yet deliver.

So we sail in this interval between the ages, in this time when old stories have vacated the throne but new ones haven't yet risen to guide our lives. Many of us experience as powerless the stories our Christian tradition offered us. Creation. Fall. Redemption. Consummation. Demythologized, each one, wounded by the rise of critical thinking about both the Bible which offered us the stories and the Christian tradition(s) which preserved and transmitted them over millennia.

Not only in their precritical form have the stories been deposed, however. Increasingly the criticism which deposed them (and the forms of the stories *it* created) is also under attack. Many are finding this route dry and unfulfilling. It doesn't let living waters, waters the Bible may offer us even now, flow freely into our parched modern lives.

What, if anything, will replace the stories in their precritical and critical forms? Can the ancient images live again? Can Adam and Eve stir again in our bones? Can we, with the Israelites, cross again the Red (precritical)/reed (critical) Sea? Can Jesus still save us, whatever salvation means in a sad and cynical age? Does a time when we'll weep no more by the waters of Babylon lie still ahead?

Who can say? We must still cross this time between the times, when the shape of the new remains unclear. How to travel across this period between the collapse of the old and the rise of the new is what this book is about. It's about what it feels like to be "postmodern" people, with all the danger and promise being "post-anything" carries with it. "Post–" carries the name of the age it succeeds but adds the "post–" to say the age has disintegrated. Its name alone is no longer enough.

We postmoderns know the name of the modern age we're leaving. We know it's no longer our home. We're beginning to grieve. But within our grief stir glimmers of the hope that beyond the postmodern there lies a new age. Someday there will again be stories to stir our souls, to light our way, to give us a home.

Why do I believe so strongly we're in a liminal age? I offer three sources: personal experience, pastoral experience, and the larger world revealed through books, magazines, newspapers, movies, personal relationships. A word about each and the role they play in this book is appropriate because they provide the raw material from which the book emerges.

A primary reason for believing our age is liminal is having experienced the world that way during my thirty-odd years of life.

My missionary parents raised me in a milieu strongly influenced by both Mennonite and fundamentalist streams of thoughts. The Mennonite stream offered strong social boundaries. We were a people set apart, called to create a haven of peace, security, and right living in an evil and threatening world. When I was young my dad wore a plain coat and my mom a plain dress and prayer veiling as visible signs of commitment to that alternate community. I set myself apart in junior high school by exercising alone in one corner of the gym while my classmates square-danced.

The fundamentalist stream offered strong intellectual and doctrinal boundaries. The Bible is the literal, inerrant Word of God. Just about everything in it is actual, historical fact, including Adam and Eve, the Great Flood, and Jonah in the whale or big fish. God is an omnipotent being (male) in the sky, a benevolent dictator we can blame or credit for whatever happens. Accepting Jesus Christ as your personal Savior brings salvation. Following this you feel the burden of sin drop away—as it does for the pilgrim Christian in *Pilgrim's Progress*. After this you abstain from smoking, drinking, swearing, and dancing. And you prepare for heaven.

This is a caricature, I know. As I proceed, I want to show that fundamentalism has a richness to offer in the voyage across trackless wastes. But that's how I experienced fundamentalism at the time.

Because I experienced it that way, I finally rebelled against it. I decided I didn't believe in God. The Bible's fabulous stories weren't true. Jesus was just an odd man. We came from no place and are going nowhere. When I encountered critical approaches to the Bible and faith in college, I concluded they supported my faithlessness.

I had entered my own liminal time, between the guiding stories of my childhood, now dead, and whatever stories might arise to replace them. I wandered lonely and cold. The stars haunted me. I wanted the guidance they seemed to offer, even as I doubted there was any home toward which they could lead me.

But gradually, without jettisoning critical insights, I began to reappropriate faith. The old stories began to move me again. My liminal time isn't over; I remain a child of my age and can't find my new home alone. Yet I find myself standing sometimes at least on the threshold, looking through the door, seeing glimmers of the new home in the distance.

Turning to the pastoral experiences that fed my conviction of living in a liminal age, I spent most of the 1980s pastoring a strange congregation, Germantown Mennonite Church. It was founded in 1683 by Quaker and Mennonite families fleeing troubles in Europe. It's the oldest Mennonite church on the American continent. Tradition therefore wells from it in a ceaseless stream. Yet during my time there, participants in this venerable church were mostly in their twenties and thirties and producing children by the bushels. We did our youthful thing while the wraiths of those long dead, the many who had preceded us over the past three centuries, fluttered around us and reminded us we had a heritage not yet willing to be forgotten.

Many attenders shared my kind of background. Whether Mennonite, Baptist, Quaker, Catholic, or Jewish, we had experienced our age as liminal. The faith of childhood had died, the faith of the future was shadowy, yet the quest for faith was sharp enough and poignant enough to bring us regularly to church. We too stood sometimes together on the threshold, suspecting we saw a home in the distance, and perhaps Jesus standing at the door, ready to welcome us in.

Then there are all the hints of liminality the world is giving out. In the United States, presidents tell us we got lost when one president did this, and another president that—but now they have found a new way. Ronald Reagan told us it was morning again in America, correctly articulating for us our sense of being lost in a featureless twilight. But even as the ever-popular actor rode his horse into the setting sun, people knew that homelessness, environmental degradation, budget woes, and more, would create tense plot lines when the sequel, with George Bush as lead, hit the screens.

In just about every feature of current life we sense the loss of old certainties. Our institutions—goverment, economy, schools, churches and synagogues, intellectual life—are faltering. But we're not sure what the antidotes are. In *Habits of the Heart* Robert Bellah and company mourned the loss of national cohesion. What would replace it? In *The Closing of the American Mind*, Allan Bloom hit a reactionary nerve when he mourned our loss of old certainties and argued that their replacement, uncertainty as prime virtue, wouldn't do the job. Even as disintegration proceeds, however, the very fact it's being recognized offers hope. Perhaps the nation stands on a threshold, ready to look for what lies on the other side.

In Canada too, the center is weak. People clash over which language they should speak. They debate budget priorities as the national budget deficit mounts. They choose religions from the pluralistic marketplace.

Around the world they crumble old certainties turned tentative by ceaseless change. Together we yearn, millions of us, to cross to the other side of our liminal time.

In the pages ahead I want to travel toward the other

side in three broad stages. First I'll describe in more detail the shape of our problem—the symbolic forty years of wilderness in which we're wandering. I'll place tentative steps toward a solution at the heart of the book. Finally I'll explore what outlines of the new home we can see, if only faintly, beyond the threshold.

Plenty of books have examined the issues I propose to discuss. Why write another? Because I believe a book is needed that relates the issues to congregational life and the struggle to make sense of contemporary life all Christians face. I want to write a book rooted in life as people who feel caught in this liminal time really live and experience it.

I *will* consult some experts as I proceed, because they have much to offer. I hope to write intelligently enough to interest a few of them, even if their response is only to tell me how very wrong I am. I'll be writing primarily, however, in the only way a nonexpert can—as one personally caught up in the dread and joy of our time.

I hope to be helpful in some small way to kindred travelers. My intended companions are all who care about congregational life and Christian identity in a pluralistic and muddled age—Christians on the way, and the teachers, preachers, and church leaders charged with offering guidance. The Questions for Discussion and Reflection at the end of each chapter make the book potentially useful for Sunday school or small-group discussions of the journey.

It may be a forlorn wish, but I'd like to reach an audience that includes both fundamentalists and people so disenchanted with a disintegrating Christianity that they put "post–"even in front of the word *Christian*. I risk being too pluralistic for the fundamentalist and too committed to a particular way for the post-Christian. But I hope to speak to both ends of the spectrum, because I need them both. We all, I believe, need them both.

A final word on method. The astute reader will note that a key tool I use to get where I want to go is dialectical reasoning. I'm hopelessly seduced by this method, which tries to hold extremes in tension. It takes polarities, opposite ends of a spectrum, and refuses to jettison either. It examines thesis and antithesis and shows how both are needed to create a synthesis greater than either. I use the method because I'm drawn to it and because it's well suited to a liminal time in which old truths *and* the reaction to them are ingredients we can use to find new truth.

The singularity of the old, old story of Jesus joined to the pluralistic reaction against all old stories can give us a new story. This story can be both new *and* Christian. It can reach out to an ever-changing world and throb still with the life of that old, old story, as John tells us.

> In the beginning was the Word, and the Word was with God, and the Word was God. . . . All things were made through him, and without him was not anything made that was made. In him was life, and the life was the light of men [and women]. The light shines in the darkness, and the darkness has not overcome it. (1:1-5, RSV)

Even in a liminal time, even as trackless wastes and eternal night threaten to swallow us, the light shines and leads us on. Where and how it might lead is what now needs exploration.

CHAPTER 1

Our Homeless Age

For centuries now, exile has stalked all of us whose homes were once the traditions and communities the modern world is busily dismantling. Perhaps it has stalked us always, even when we were wandering nomads, our homes the deserts and the wild lands and we loved the old ways destroyed by the coming of agriculture and the rise of cities. Ever since the first days, perhaps, grandmothers and grandfathers have sat misty-eyed by their fires, telling of when they were young and life was good, so good, so much better than today. Always, perhaps, has the angel's flaming sword flashed against homesick souls trying to reenter Eden.

Perhaps so, but after we peel away the forms of exile that have accompanied us from the beginning, a fiercer strain of exile than faced our ancestors stands revealed. Now not only a people here, a community there, a tribe somewhere else—afflicted by the normal cycles of history—are being exiled. Now those longing to return home aren't only Native Americans, black descendants of slaves wrenched from African homelands, wandering Jews, members of ethnic subcultures disintegrating after only a few generations in America.

Now, in the midst of decades labeled "Age of Me" or "Age of Greed," the longing ones are all of us. We're plagued by crime and AIDS and crack. We're bombarded every day by news of guns in classrooms and babies found in bags or stuffed in trash cans. We wonder what happened to close-knit, small-town America. We yearn for a center that can hold. But we can't agree on what the center should be. "As the twentieth century approaches its end," says Christopher Lasch, "the conviction grows that many other things are ending too. Storm warnings, portents, hints of catastrophe haunt our times."[1]

We can find a home, I believe, even if not the one we left. Looking for that home is this book's project. But in this chapter I'll resist yearning toward home. I'll address, instead, the shape of our homelessness, of our liminal existence between old and new.

The first major section will examine the texture of our homeless age and the forces that created and characterize it. To clear the way for the new possibilities addressed in the rest of the book, a second section will present and critique two common responses to homelessness. One is the attempt to maintain old homes in the midst of the era's muddle. The other is the belief that the muddle itself can be home.

THE HOMELESS AGE

I hope to converse through this book with people of many traditions. But in this section and throughout, Mennonites will make frequent appearances, for several reasons.

First, I'm Mennonite, which inevitably shapes my perspective.

Second, I'm writing for Herald Press, a Mennonite publisher whose audience includes a large contingent of Mennonites.

Third, I'll be trying to show how a particular identity, such as my Mennonite one, can offer a perspective enriching to all. And so, instead of trying to departicularize my viewpoint, turning it colorless and bland and traditionless to reach a broad audience, I'll instead particularize it. I'll try to use the color and vigor and struggle present in my tradition to model in my writing one way of bringing particularity and plurality into fruitful relationship.

Finally, it took many cultures and subcultures centuries to travel from tradition to modernity. Mennonites have compressed the voyage into a few recent generations. We have not only undergone all the pressures present in the larger culture but have experienced them in an intensified and abbreviated way. We thus offer a tightly focused lens through which to view the dynamics of the contemporary world.

The Homeless Age and the Mennonite Experience

So intense has Mennonite experience been that (as I noted in my introduction) my brief, thirty-odd years of life have spanned two distinct eras. During the first one, we were largely isolated from the larger world. Now, as an article title in our church magazine put it, "We're headed for a crisis." This refers to a crisis in worship patterns caused by the arrival of new people from non-Mennonite backgrounds. They bring with them and need forms of worship the church may be hard-pressed to accommodate.[2]

What factors underlie this experience? As Beulah S. Hostetler understands it, in America the late nineteenth century was a time in which not only Mennonites, but all Christians trying to remain separate from the dominant culture, experienced stress. One cause of stress was the modernistic theology fundamentalism reacted against. Also stressful were the changes in social and economic structures which "threatened the continuing existence of small, self-regulated communities which prior to 1870 had been a dominant feature . . . of American society."

The Mennonite Church, including the eastern Pennsylvania wing Hostetler focuses on, reacted with what

Hostetler calls "defensive structuring and codification of practice." Expressions of this included a high rate of marriage within the group, strong authoritarian control, limitations on association with outside groups, and adoption of cultural identity symbols.[3]

E. M. Wardle's comments, though contemporary, capture the flavor of that era. "Our women are to be modest in dress, non-preachers, faithfully and submissively rearing their children, loving their husbands. . . . Each [man] should love his wife dearly, and support his family financially."[4]

Back then, one knew women preachers, house-husbands, jewelry, unions, voting, fighting (whether in war or against classmates), and most musical instruments were wrong.

One knew what was right: Following Jesus according to the Sermon on the Mount. Uttering no oaths because Jesus said your yes should be yes and your no, no. Not resisting a request for your stereo but giving your TV, as well. Taking the Bible *seriously*, which meant reading it and praying over it every day. Living meekly and humbly and uprightly in the land. And one knew who decided right and wrong: the ministers and bishops of the church.

Then it all crumbled. Hostetler says:

> In the quarter century following 1950, virtually all of the elements of defensive structuring disappeared from Mennonite practice. During the period of sloughing off of cultural identity symbols it appeared to some Mennonites that their only difference from Protestant neighbors was a certain inability to articulate beliefs.[5]

In some parts of the Mennonite Church (including my own extended family), the old home, securely bounded by the old defensive structures and codified practices, remains.

Others of us wander now in exile. We see the old

ways as quietist, too withdrawn and sectarian, unable to meet the challenges of the present age. We've rejected those key cultural identity symbols, the male plain coat and the covering women once wore to symbolize submission to God and man. Unions are ways to empower the powerless. Nonvoting Mennonites are now on the wrong side. We charge them with privatistic withdrawal from the public arena, a withdrawal which supports an unjust status quo.

We still don't go to war, mostly, but talk to some of us about whether violence is justified in South Africa or Central America. We hedge, quick to avoid judging means for liberation used by oppressed people in whose shoes we haven't walked. And musical instruments? Wrong? Did you say wrong? We don't even know who decides right and wrong for us anymore. The ministers and bishops don't. They serve the group and carry out its will. They don't impose decisions from above.

I once attended a general assembly of Mennonites who had gathered in the thousands to conduct church business, worship together, and nurture a denominational sense of family. Later I reported my impressions:

> I worshiped with who you [the Mennonite Church] are today, there in the Elliott Hall of Music. I looked around. A handful of plain coats. A scattering of coverings. The women's hair cut. . . . Some men in shorts and sandals. Youth everywhere, youth who remember not what I remember, who certainly show little outward evidence of being Mennonite, gearing up to tell me how outdated I am when I've barely gotten done telling my parents the same. And onstage . . . oh, onstage! Big black boxes hooked up to awesome amplifiers. Guitars. Electric basses. Saxophones. And more. Then the music, booming, thumping, dancing out. . . .[6]

How did we get here? How did all of us, no matter

who we are, get from where we were to where we are? The authors of *Habits of the Heart* subtitled it *Individualism and Commitment in American Life*. Then they mourned the rise of individualism to a chilling peak and yearned, often wistfully, for new forms of commitment whose shapes don't quite come clear. How did the traditions that bound us, shaped us, and sheltered us so weaken that not only I—who grew up in a tightly bounded little subculture—sense the loss of home, but also these experts, speaking for a broad national culture?

I want to offer six oversimplified answers: secularization, modern transportation and communication, plurality and pluralism, relativism, individualism, and loss of authority. These forces have a positive side which I'll examine later. Now I want to inspect their role as wrecking balls shattering the walls of our old homes.

Secularization

In traditional homes, life unfolds under what Peter Berger calls the "sacred canopy," or within a "sacred home." In the traditional Mennonite home, you knew what clothes to put on in the morning: plain ones. You knew what was forbidden: any corrupting contact with the larger world. The tightly knit life of the community was held together by shared symbols drawn from the Bible, old hymns, and common Mennonite practice. Worshiping, praying, singing, working, and eating together added more glue. You knew what your role was—one kind for a woman, another for a man. You knew whom to marry—another Mennonite. Right and wrong were cleanly cleaved.

When I ripped a picture of dubious content from a magazine of dubious worth, scraps of which were later found and identified by higher authorities in my life, I instantly knew my transgression was grave. I had violated the boundaries of my sacred home, that overarching structure of thinking, acting, feeling, and being within which I lived as a Mennonite boy.

The boundaries were different, perhaps, but members of the traditional European, Native American, African, Asian, or Latin cultures from which most North Americans came would have felt similarly enclosed within an all-encompassing house of being. Such houses were built on a structure of respect for sacred books, traditions, or persons who were beyond question.

Then came secularization. "By secularization," says Peter Berger, "we mean the process by which sectors of society and culture are removed from the domination of religious institutions and symbols."[7] When secularization came along, it asked questions: "Why is this sacred? Who says this behavior is wrong and that one right? Why can't I look at this picture?" Aided by a scientific method that accepted as real and meaningful only what could be empirically tested, a wave of secularization began to spread around the world from the fifteenth century on.

William H. Willimon gives a vivid example of what happens to the sacred home as secularization undercuts it. Looking back, he says, he perceives that "a momentous event in my faith journey occurred on a Sunday evening in 1963 in Greenville, South Carolina, when, in defiance of the state's archaic Blue Laws, the Fox Theater opened on Sunday." He and six other good young Methodists sneaked out of church and into the theater. This, Willimon says, "symbolized a watershed in the history of Christianity in the United States. On that night . . . the last pocket of resistance to secularity in the Western world . . . served notice that it would no longer be a prop for the church."[8]

On that night, and on so many others since science and reason and enlightened thinking arose, religion gave up one more sector of influence. Secularized society forced it deeper into the reservation set aside for it. It became a domesticated animal for people to enjoy from their car windows, while remembering the days when it ran wild and free across the sweeping grasslands.

Modern Transportation and Communication

Secularization was powerful enough as a philosophical undercurrent stimulating the scientific revolution, the Enlightenment, and the industrial revolution. Once modern transportation and communication spread around the globe, it couldn't be stopped. It was carried everywhere by easy travel and electronic signals blanketing the world. Few cultures or traditions escaped contact with the idea that the truest reality was defined by scientific study. When even cloistered living rooms flickered in TV light, things changed forever. This free travel of people and ideas helped create the four remaining forces.

Plurality and Pluralism

Plurality as a condition and *pluralism* as ideology, or way of thinking, intertwine to deepen our exile. We often interchange plurality and pluralism. This obscures their differences.[9] *Plurality* refers to the simple existence today of many different cultures, traditions, religions, lifestyles, ways of looking at things. This is an inescapable part of contemporary life for all but dwellers in the most isolated corners of the world. (And there must not be many of them, judging from pictures we've seen over the years of even the most primitive tribespeople holding transistor radios to their ears.)

The plurality we experience every day, particularly in the urban settings we increasingly inhabit, contributes to a cycle of experiencing and thinking which fosters an ideology of *pluralism*. Pluralism is a way of thinking about the world which, taking plurality into account, believes there may be many ways of making sense of life. I've opened myself to a form of pluralistic ideology by accepting that my own are not the only valid truths. I accept that I live in a world in which my truths don't form a sacred canopy under which everyone else will happily nestle.

A pluralistic ideology no doubt feeds, in turn, sensitivity to plurality. Openness to many truths can help eyes see the rich and variegated fabric of customs and perspectives humanity is weaving.

Unfortunately, this cycle of plurality and pluralism can create an atomized, broken society in which no culture, community, tradition, or institution can speak for any truth larger than its own narrow slice. Each provides its own justification for its existence and style of operating. None can appeal to a larger set of basic principles agreed to by all.[10]

To the extent we dwellers in a pluralistic setting find a home, then, it's often small and unsatisfying—a home our small group, or even we ourselves, construct. We no longer know where to find a large, wondrous, cosmos-encompassing home as large as the universe.

Relativism

As a missionary kid, I experienced a plurality of cultures and religions. This pushed me toward pluralistic ideology. That degenerated into relativism. I concluded that the presence of many possible truths suggested there might be *no* truth better than another, and therefore no ultimate truth.

Relativism says we have only the shifting and insubstantial truths that arise in each situation as ways of organizing and making sense of reality. But that's all they are—necessary social conveniences. Truth is dependent on, or *relative* to, particular cultures, religions, situations, people. This means my truth is my truth, your truth is your truth. If at points they intersect, that's great. But whether they do or do not doesn't matter. Truth is simply what you make it. That's not much of a wall for a sacred home.

Individualism

Pluralism and relativism can lead us to think truths are as numerous as people. In the religious realm, this can lead people to forsake the large, intricate structure of Christianity, which has nurtured millions for millennia under a common roof, for their own personal religion. Bellah and company note that "today religion in America is as private and diverse as New England colonial religion was public and unified." They tell of Sheila, who has named her religion, or faith, after herself, and calls it Sheilaism. Her truth is her "own little voice." As the authors rightly say, "This suggests the logical possibility of over 220 million American religions, one for each of us."[11]

Pluralism and relativism are not the only sources of such individualism, which has many roots. Bellah and company believe four traditions—biblical, civic, utilitarian, and expressive—contribute to American individualism. They note that, although each has made distinctive contributions, they unite in one commonality: "We believe in the dignity, indeed the sacredness of the individual." This belief "lies at the very core of American culture." The authors don't completely oppose individualism, which they see as a source of American greatness. But they do see it as sapping America of a communal spirit, of the ability to gather around any common values other than each person's right to choose his or her own values.[12]

Loss of Authority

As the exiling forces batter old homes, they undercut traditional forms of authority. Bible, church, state;

pope, priest, minister; mayor, senator, president—all are weakened. Authority, if present anywhere outside the individual, resides perhaps in science, which determines the laws and regularities that undergird life.

But even science carries less authority than it once did. The twentieth century gave physics "Heisenberg's uncertainty principle." It states that what the physicist sees is inevitably tainted by the very act of observation. This suggests that not even the scientist can get at life's pure, objective data.

The point of view popularized by books like Thomas Kuhn's *The Structure of Scientific Revolutions* moves in the same direction. To oversimplify, this perspective talks of "paradigms" and "paradigm shifts." It then suggests that the paradigm, or overarching worldview of the scientist, controls what the scientist finds. One could say that the scientist is usually able to see and find only what he or she is looking for.

The old homes built on a hierarchical, master-slave form of authority may be forever gone, except in isolated quarters. This isn't all bad, this crumbling of the power of Papa and Mama church or state—who fed us, took care of us, and kept us warm in exchange for unquestioning obedience. Until better forms of authority arise, however, the loss of old ones contributes to our exile.

I felt such exile stalking me every day during my years as an urban pastor. When I preached I recognized that in my setting, at least, the Bible from which I preached was a weak authority. To stand with Billy Graham and proclaim, "The Bible says!" wasn't enough. I could see the wheels turning in the heads of my secularized listeners. "Oh, really? The Bible says? What does this 'we're all sinners' business have to do with Carl Rogers and unconditional acceptance? Jesus rose? But science says. . . ."

The issue was sometimes my authority versus theirs.

"Sure, the Bible may say that to him, but has he walked in my shoes? *This* is what the Bible says to me and it's equally valid." Or pluralism and relativism interacted to yield, "Jesus is the one way? You must be kidding! What about Buddhism and Judaism and Jungian psychology? I mean, is any way better than any other? Let's not be provincial or triumphalist in the way we relate to other truths, which deserve our respect." On the other hand, there were those who felt the walls of the home were all too flimsy. They called for more biblical preaching, for deeper commitment to Jesus' gospel. The others told them, "Fine, that's okay for you, I respect your walk, but don't lay it on me."

TWO ATTEMPTS TO FIND A HOME

I'm not the only person who senses we're living in a liminal age in which the old ways don't work properly. Countless people sense this and have tried to address the problem. Although both secular and Christian strategies exist, I'll be focusing on the Christian ones to keep the scope of my discussion manageable.

I want to briefly summarize and critique two opposing Christian strategies which offer the raw material I'll later try to combine into a richer whole. My summary won't properly capture the complexity of Christian options in North America. It will, however, identify the two opposing poles around which discussions of ways of being Christian often revolve. I'll call the one *separatism*, the other *translationism*.

Separatism is often synonymous with fundamentalism; and translationism with liberalism. However, I avoid using *fundamentalism* or *liberalism* as my labels. This is because I want to focus on tendencies that are usually, *but not always*, associated with the groups these labels name. I want to be free to focus on a tendency without referring automatically to a particular set of people.

Separatism

My treatment of the Mennonite fundamentalist experience introduced a variety of separatist leanings. Now I want to examine more closely four strategies separatist groups often use to maintain a home.

Separate Basis of Authority

First is a separate basis of authority. Rightly sensing that secularization threatens the sacred home's walls, the separatist tries to establish authorities separate from—and often opposed to—the larger evil world's authorities. Separatist authorities include the Bible, the preacher, or the norms of the group. Separatists try not to care what psychologists, sociologists, politicians, or the mass media are saying. They're not authoritative.

Separatists often revere the Bible as *the* infallible source of guidance. One is to memorize it, to quote it at mealtimes, to live and breathe and drink and eat it. When questions of right thinking, feeling, living, or anything at all arise, its authority far outweighs anything the secular world can offer.

Separate Ways of Thinking and Feeling

Separate ways of thinking and feeling flow logically from commitment to separate authorities. Biblical precepts and the pure doctrine of the one true faith are to dominate ways of thinking about and experiencing the world.

Among fundamentalist or conservative evangelical separatists, walls of the doctrinal home often include the following: Consciousness of sin. The atoning power of the cross. Salvation offered by Jesus Christ, true man but even more truly God, born of a virgin. The clean living appropriate to the saved. And the hope of heaven, offered by Jesus, who will return on clouds of glory to gather the redeemed.

To maintain a separated life within such walls, one

must keep out the world. Secular books, radio, television—all can taint clean minds and bodies and emotions. I was forbidden to read comics for this reason. My worst boyhood day came when (consciousness of sin having grown too heavy to bear) I confessed to my mother the double sin of stealing grocery money and using it to buy a majestic stack of Superman comics.

Separate Social Life
A separate social life is a natural companion of a separate thinking and feeling life. Separatists are birds who flock together. They create churches, private schools ranging from elementary through seminary, and other social settings. These make it at least theoretically possible to avoid meaningful contact with the outside world from the cradle to the grave. James Barr describes the "informal but . . . profound way" fundamentalists maintain true doctrine and practice.

> The hearing of speakers, the discussion of difficulties, meetings for prayer and Bible study groups, evangelistic activity towards the non-believer and the informal fellowship of the group all build up together a powerful and sensitive consciousness of what is "sound" doctrine and real Christianity.[13]

Separation Through Conversion
One enters the life set apart in these ways through conversion. This is the fourth area of separation. Not all groups practice stereotypical, revival-tent, and sawdust-trail conversion. Most do, however, provide some ritual drawing a line between those who remain in the world and those who join the separatist home.

Conversion is one such ritual. If you don't convert, if you don't make a conscious decision to accept Jesus Christ as personal Savior, if you don't make a commitment to separation—then you don't truly belong in the sacred home. Because separatists need to maintain some form of alternate living, this is understandable. To keep the larger decaying society at bay, you have to know who's in and who's out.

Critiquing Separatism

Many Christians who grew up in sacred homes, then left them for the intoxicating freedoms of the big bad wonderful world, are homesick for the good old walls. The strength of separatism is its passionate effort, against all the daunting odds, to meet this eternal human need for a safe, warm, and sacred home.

Separatism tries to do this by creating an alternative, separate way of structuring life to supply what's missing in the outside world. Separatism often does manage to build a grand old house. Made of sturdy wood and brick, its lines noble and compelling, it invites our homesick hearts to enter and sit by the fire for a spell.

Unfortunately, separatism's efforts are usually unsustainable. Separatists are repeatedly assimilated into the dominant culture. Standing against the outside world's incessant pressures proves too daunting. Too many tourists flock to Lancaster County, Pennsylvania, and overwhelm traditional Amish ways. Or fundamentalists and their TV preachers yield to the gospel of success and wealth the larger culture dangles seductively before them.

The structure collapses from within, as well, because separatism's need to enforce a strict conformity held in check by rigid authority fosters a narrowing and darkening of life. This makes the light of secularism, when it encroaches, intensely appealing. Rebellion erupts. Individuals leave the group or challenge it from within. Whole groups, sometimes, liberalize.

Separatism risks being a house built on sand, the unacknowledged, shifting sand of modernity. Separatism's sacred house, beautiful though it is, sinks slowly into the sand. The sea crashes around it, and who knows when a fierce hurricane will topple the majestic structure into the waves?

Translationism

The opposite response to exile we might call translationism. Its strategies involve living in the world as it really is—modern warts, shifting sand, and all. It then works at *translating* the gospel into those terms. Translationism turns upside down the separatist approach, converting the areas of separation into four areas of translation. Mainline liberalism often exemplifies the translationist style. But the tendency is broader than liberalism. It appears wherever Christian groups try to translate the gospel into secular forms.

Translated Understanding of Authority

The first area of translation is authority. Translationists like secularization's dethroning of traditional authorities. Translationists are comfortable with critical probing of Scripture or other religious authorities. They accept critical scholarship, which uses, as the foundation for studying all authorities, the one authority secularization allows as their critical, scientific methodology.

When translationism critically dissects the Bible, it sifts through Scripture for insights translatable into modern thinking. It then doubts the value of the rest. I see this in my own translationist-tinged relationship with the Bible. Take Jesus' miracles and their meaning for me today. Critical scholarship says Jesus' status as miracle-worker wasn't a unique one in his day. This tempts me to conclude the Gospel writers simply stuck Jesus into a framework or pigeonhole familiar to them, called "miracle-worker." Then they showed how he was, yes, a miracle-worker, only not a run-of-the-mill one.

These writers were operating in this prescientific

framework in which miracles weren't the odd things they are today. Once you run their words through the sieve of modern scientific understandings, you have to assume nothing that really disrupted scientific law could have happened back then, no matter what it sounds like. If I read the account of Jesus stilling a storm through translationist glasses, I have to work hard to find anything authoritative in it.

Translated Ways of Thinking and Feeling

Translated ways of thinking and feeling are a second area. As translationism has faced the many streams of thought that have emerged in this century, it has tried to translate the faith into them. Harvey Cox's *The Secular City* offers a noteworthy 1960s example. The title says it. Cox values the good of secularizing, urbanizing society. He wants to show how Christianity is compatible with it.

The 1960s "death of God" movement had a similar aim. John A. T. Robinson was one of the early popularizers of a perspective later emblazoned on the famous *Time* cover as the question, "Is God Dead?" He once deeply influenced my thinking. When I was leaving behind my own fundamentalist-Mennonite home of being, Robinson placed me on the threshold of adventure. I gazed at open fields and a lane winding out to the whole wide world when I read words like these: "The signs are that we are reaching the point at which the whole conception of a God 'out there,' which has served us so well since the collapse of the three-decker universe, is itself becoming more of a hindrance than a help." Maybe, Robinson speculates, "the Freudians are right, that such a God—the God of traditional popular theology—is a projection, and perhaps we are being called to live without that projection in any form."[14]

During that era we were being called, thought Robinson, to live with a God who made sense from within a way of thinking shaped by the six forces of modernity. Though continuing evolution of theological fashion has resurrected God for many, Robinson still speaks to anyone trying to hold God and secular thought somehow together.

Two important contemporary translation efforts involve Liberation Theology and "New Age" ways of thinking. Liberation Theology translates the gospel into historical categories. It shows how God is at work in this and that pattern in history, particularly where poverty and oppression are rampant. New Age thinking often degenerates into an occultist, pantheistic mush. But it properly argues for renewed appreciation of the feminine, the nonrational, and emotional, the basic linkage of all life. Matthew Fox's project in *The Original Blessing* is to create a Christianity appreciative of such values.

Theological, biblical, or religious concepts considered archaic are often translated into social-scientific language. David Martin, speaking of various responses to secularism, makes an applicable comment. "The committed Christian . . . may translate Christian concepts into secular equivalents: communion-community, sin-alienation, holiness-wholeness." Mainline liberal clergy translationists often reduce Christianity to psychotherapeutic terms. "Freudian and Jungian psychological mythology partly replaces and partly parallels the tenets of Christian theology."[15]

I plead guilty. Such language is a tool I often use to make the gospel meaningful to myself and others in the modern age. Debiblicized words roll most smoothly off my tongue. Sin? I wince. I prefer fragmentation. Salvation? I wince again. How about individuation, integration, or wholeness?

Translated Social Life

A translated social life is a third tendency. To borrow from Ernest Troeltsch's time-honored typology, translationists form churches, not sects, like separatists do. And churches translate themselves into social styles compatible with the larger society. Indeed, translationist churches often *are* the larger society. Membership in such churches and in larger society is often part of the same fabric of things. Witness Episcopalian George Bush.

Assimilation

Finally, one joins translationist churches more by assimilation than by conversion. Such churches do have membership rolls and general requirements. But since clear lines between church and world aren't drawn, the sharp demarcation offered by conversion or similar rituals is less important. During my early, translationist-tinged years of pastoring, I thought an adequate system for taking in members was making vague statements about congregational goals and letting people seep in by osmosis.

Critiquing Translationism

The strength of translationism is its aim to build a house on the rock of the modern era. And the modern era *is* rich. Translationism says, "On this rock, this reality squarely faced, we'll build our church." It's right to build on that rock. Constructing a sacred home without taking account of modernity *is* building on sand. Translationism can interact productively with contemporary sciences, philosophies, arts, and anything else the secular world offers. It can show linkages between Christianity and secular concerns, benefiting both.

What translationism risks, however, is waking someday to the reality that the rock is bare. It says, "If we just take these old Christian materials and translate them into modern terms, we'll have ourselves a house." But if the translation is too thorough, there won't be a house. It will have been translated away, leaving only the modern age, which by itself offers poor shelter.

And so the rock of translationism rises rough and solid by the sea, at home in the wind and the waves. No hurricane can do more than wash over it, then leave it behind, intact. But those who long for more than camping on rocks will find this weak comfort.

Separatism and translationism. Flawed but offering, each of them, unique richness and strength. Can they be linked? Yes, I think, and in the pages ahead I'll try to explain how.

QUESTIONS FOR DISCUSSION AND REFLECTION

1. What good and what bad things do separatism and translationism each offer us?

2. Who will prepare the star charts to guide us across our trackless wastes during this interval between the collapse of the old age and the rise of the next?

3. Can there be a return to authority?

4. Is there a home to be found?

5. If there *is* a home to be found, will we Christians carry on a thoroughly separatist discussion, purely for our own benefit? Or will we also work at a translationist agenda that can benefit the larger world?

6. If Christians decide to address issues in the broadest kind of way, will it matter? Will the larger world care? Or will Christians be just one more interest group trying to be heard in a pluralistic, fragmented world?

7. Can Christianity ever be truly Christian *and* the dominant force in society?

8. Should Christians create alternate communities that exist at a tangent to the larger world but are still witnesses to it?

9. Will Christians travel only as individuals, or also in communities?

10. Can translationism and separatism join forces?

CHAPTER 2

The Bible and Tradition: Three Approaches

In my first chapter I touched on the crisis of authority caused by the modernizing forces. Now I want to focus on ways the modernizing forces have affected our highest authority—the Bible. To a lesser extent, because I accept the Protestant/Mennonite commitment to let biblical authority test tradition, I'll also examine questions of authority and Christian tradition.

First I want to summarize two competing views of biblical authority and interpretation which I'll call precritical and critical. Then I'll propose ways the two might, instead of remaining the eternal antagonists exemplified below, marry to form a "postcritical" alternative.

Each year, in countless Christian colleges and seminaries affected by critical thinking, a great drama unfolds. The setting is the first Bible course of the first semester. It focuses on the Old Testament, because that, of course, is where you begin. The students shuffle in. They come, many of them from good Christian homes and good Christian churches. They don't always think and do good Christian things, but they know what they *should* think and do to be good. This course, they assume, will only deepen their knowing and turn sagging faith firm.

The class begins. The professor identifies two distinct creation accounts in Genesis. There is a theory that may account for this. It goes by such names as "documentary hypothesis" or "source theory." It holds that the Old Testament was stitched together from a variety of sources. Sources might include oral tradition, passed down from generation to generation, and various written documents. Redactors, or editors, then polished them into the form handed down to us.

Student minds reel. "Moses!" suddenly cries the possessor of a particularly astute mind. "What about Moses? Didn't he write the Pentateuch?" The professor confesses (if diplomatic) or thunders (if dogmatic) that source theory and Mosaic authorship are mutually exclusive.

The course continues. The famous Red Sea/reed sea exchange is made. Maybe the Israelites actually crossed a shallow, marshy, reedy area of the Gulf of Suez, Lake Timsah, or Lake Sirbonis. Maybe they crossed on a sandbar. Maybe a strong wind, raging at just the right moment, drove the water through the sandbar and onto the wretched Egyptians. Certainly this is more likely than that the Red Sea parted, and the Israelites crossed between those Cecil B. de Mille walls of water held back by God, the great magician.

Moving on, there is some question as to how firm a presence Satan can claim to have in an Old Testament that refers only rarely to him. Maybe people pay more attention to what they *think* the Old Testament says about Satan than to what it actually does. The professor hints Satan may not literally exist.

They keep coming, these bombshells, one or more a day. Soon the students launch a counterattack. The professor, concerned students charge, is a heretic. They say this to each other. They hurl it in the professor's face. They tell it to the school's administrators. They cry it out to their parents, who call the dean and make some comments about future alumni contributions.

A CLASH OF PARADIGMS

The drama is caused by a clash of paradigms, perspectives, or (to use Hans Küng's synonym) "models of understanding."[1] The students have been nurtured in a precritical model of biblical understanding. The professor is committed to a critical one. Each paradigm is a kind of lens. Each lens is ground according to certain specifications and comes in a particular tint. Each is thought to offer *the* correct view of things.

The stakes are high. No matter which lens people choose, the crucial vista they're trying to glimpse through it is a reliable, guiding authority. No wonder drama erupts in the classroom. When students who grew up looking through a precritical lens face suddenly the critical one, they feel betrayed. The lens imposed on them reveals an alien universe whose unfamiliar stars offer false guidance.

Now typically this clash of paradigms is resolved by making them fight each other to the death. One paradigm wins. The loser is forever rejected. Certain students will undergo a "paradigm change"[2] and ally themselves with the professor's lens. They may now consider themselves superior to their fuddy-duddy, reactionary classmates. They may not understand how they ever looked at life through such outdated spectacles. Others will glue on permanently the old paradigm, the old lens, and refuse all efforts to be pried away from it during their school careers. They will later return to family and church pledged to fight forever the heresy that almost stole their clear-eyed faith away.

Not only classmates who chose different lenses experience this rift. It runs through many Christian groups. It tears whole denominations apart, as the well-publicized war between Southern Baptist fundamentalists and moderates attests. Is there no alternative but to choose sides and fight it out? I think there is. It involves respecting and marrying the best of both viewpoints. Before marrying them, however, let me examine more closely the antagonists.

Precritical Understandings of the Bible

When I speak of precritical understandings, I mean simply any viewpoint that tries to remain uncontaminated by critical perspectives. Precritics are those who still strive to maintain a strong sacred biblical home.

I think this does reasonable justice to the way the average nonexpert experiences the issues, but it oversimplifies what's actually going. At least in North America, there must remain few Christians who are simply innocent folk not yet forced out of Eden into the modern world. What exist instead are Christians who, aware that the snake of modernity has entered the world, are trying to vanquish it. *Anticritical* might better name them. Their stance is as much reaction against modernity as simple adherence to old tradition.

The battle over biblical inerrancy, visible in books like Harold Lindsell's *Battle for the Bible*, exemplifies this. The Bible, of course, doesn't call itself inerrant. The attempt to show that it so considers itself is a modern phenomenon, prompted by perceived critical attacks on the Bible's authority. Jack Rogers and Donald McKim note there is no evidence that the English word *inerrant* existed before 1652 when the "Age of Reason" was replacing the "Age of Faith."[3]

I'll keep the term *precritical*, because it does hint at an innocent, positive quality inherent in this stance. It preserves the "foundations of the central Christian tradition" and its understanding of biblical authority.[4] I value that quality and want to show its strengths as I proceed.

Now what are key characteristics of the precritical stance? There are many, and many ways of labeling them. I suggest six: direct divine inspiration, timelessness, open universe, simplicity, piety, high authority.

Direct Divine Inspiration

"The Bible says . . .!" How many thousands of times must Billy Graham have thundered this favorite incantation. The Bible says . . . and what it says is authoritative. It rewards unquestioning trust. You can count on it. The assumption behind Graham's words is that you can trust the Bible because God, in effect, wrote it.

This isn't to accuse Graham of a simplistic theory of mechanical dictation. I doubt Graham means the biblical human author might as well be the computer terminal on which God types. Still, in this understanding, there's a direct connection between God's "pen" and the Bible's words. Paul Little (after rejecting the dictation theory) puts it this way: "God worked through the instrumentality of human personality but so guided and controlled men that what they wrote is *what He wanted written*."[5]

Timelessness

In its purest forms, the precritical stance assumes that the Bible's message is virtually timeless. When God gave Moses the Ten Commandments, God was giving them to the Israelites, yes. But God was as surely giving them to us. When God inspired Paul's view that the Corinthian women's hair should be long and covered, God was addressing them *and* us. When God, in various texts, condemns homosexuality, God might as well be sitting at a gay bar telling its patrons how things stand. Understanding the historical and cultural settings Scripture first addressed isn't ruled out—if the intent is merely to better understand what God was saying. Woe be unto anyone, however, who dares consider this or that principle nonbinding because it addressed only a long-gone situation.

The effect (and it's a very attractive one indeed) is to make the Bible seem instantly accessible, even over millennia, to the weary pilgrim turning to its pages for nurture and guidance. "Jesus is speaking to me," thinks the pilgrim, "when he warns that the cock will crow three times to mark Peter's betrayal. I betrayed Jesus today, when my co-workers mocked born-again Christians, and I sat silent with my coffee." Then the pilgrim finds forgiveness when Jesus asks, "Do you love me?" And new hope comes when Jesus tells her that, though she has betrayed, still she is called to feed Jesus' sheep.

Open Universe
There are various precritical understandings of God's power to work in the world. Some are rooted in an innocent belief that God is omnipotent. Anything God wants, God can do. More sophisticated philosophical arguments aim to show that events caused by God, but unexplainable by science or common sense, are nevertheless credible. Beyond the variations, one feature is constant: the world, the universe, all reality, is *open*. Anything can happen, not just what this science, that philosophy, or this mentality says can happen. Mark Knoll captures this understanding.

> Evangelicals believe in the reality of the transcendent and the possibility of the supernatural. This conviction, which was an unquestioned part of Christian tradition more generally until the eighteenth century, has been in the forefront of evangelical concerns.... Time and again the same note is heard: It is irresponsible, academically as well as religiously, to rule out the supernatural when considering the Scriptures.[6]

This allows precritics to interpret many biblical miracles as literal accounts.

Simplicity
This feature is tied to the preceding ones. If God as author of Scripture produced a relatively timeless

guide to living, then the process of interpreting it can be relatively simple. One needn't know Greek, or care that a hypothetical document called "Q" may lie behind the shaping of the synoptic Gospels, to be challenged by them. Those with fancy degrees can provide good translations and clarify muddy areas (if all that education hasn't messed them up), but one needs no degrees to hear God's Word.

This understanding minimizes the rift between high priests of academia and peons in the pews which yawns wide in Christian circles dominated by critical thought. Noll notes that "while the evangelical community respects its scholars, it also expects them to communicate the results of research in a style that is both understandable and supports treasured beliefs."[7]

Piety

Affirmation of piety contributes to simplicity of interpretation. Rogers and McKim suggest that the early Christians experienced the Bible as authoritative guide by the power of "the Holy Spirit working in their hearts." The Reformers, according to Robert M. Grant, held similar beliefs. "By the light of the Spirit . . . the religious value of Scripture could be at once defined and transmitted."[8] The precritical lens preserves such viewpoints, seeing a pious openness to the Holy Spirit's work in one's heart and experience as a crucial part of biblical interpretation and application.

This underlies devotional study of Scripture, in which individuals or groups pray and study passages and share how God speaks through them. Paul Tillich spent his life trying to show "correlations" between Scripture's past and present meanings. Complex philosophical, theological, psychological thinking, and more aided his project. For precritics, simple Spirit-led piety offers the correlations and builds the bridges between then and now.

High Authority

Suppose you have a book whose timeless words were spoken by the God who created a universe in which anything can happen. Suppose God's very Spirit works in human hearts to interpret those words to anyone, regardless of learning. Then you have a very important book which offers utterly trustworthy guidance through the snares and cares of this vale of tears. You have a book which deserves to exercise highest authority over your life.

This is the precritics' Bible. It's the Bible Mennonites have mostly owned. This Bible often makes a dramatic impact on the lives of its possessors—or more accurately, perhaps, those possessed by it. My ancestors were thus possessed. Thousands went to their graves, burned and drowned by persecutors who saw treason in their rejection of infant baptism and refusal to bear arms.

Precritical Understandings of Tradition

At least in my Mennonite/Protestant experience, shaped by the Reformed affirmation of Scripture as highest authority, precritical understandings of tradition are more implicit than precritical understandings of the Bible. They're voiced informally, if at all. To the extent they exist, however, what I've said about precritics and the Bible applies also to precritics and tradition. The key feature is the assumption of a direct, timeless, simple connection between past and present.

Precritical Mennonites exemplify this in relation to both the larger Christian tradition and their own Mennonite one, with its roots in sixteenth-century Anabaptism. Suppose questions of church polity arise. Should there be deacons or elders? What role should a pastor fill? An important first step has been to turn to Acts, or a Pauline letter, and let the biblical patterns of church organization shape contemporary patterns as fully and directly as possible.

If one needs more clarity, guidance may come from the Anabaptist vision. This vision supposedly began in 1525 in Switzerland (with the rebaptism of adults) and proceeded in a relatively direct line to Mennonites in North America. One can move easily back and forth, looking for lessons from past centuries and applying them in the present with minimal translation.

Critical Understandings of the Bible

My treatment of critical understandings will again oversimplify complex currents. But I think a reasonably fair picture of critical trends emerges by contrasting precritical characteristics with their critical counterparts. I'll call them human mediation of inspiration, historicism, semi-closed universe, complexity, rationality, and mixed authority.

Human Mediation of Inspiration

The critical counterpart to direct divine inspiration is the human mediation of inspiration. According to critical thought, people played a crucial role in shaping the Bible. Various oral and written traditions, whose origins are often lost in the mists of time, provided raw material. Over thousands of years, in ways too complex for full understanding, countless authors and editors shaped and reshaped this material to give us the Bible we know.

In this view, people are inextricably woven into the Bible's creation. How then does inspiration happen? This is a much "iffier" matter for critics than for precritics. For some, the human element expands to fill the entire Bible. This leaves no room for God's voice. The Bible becomes a human book along with other human books—great, yes, but human.

There are other options. One understanding is that God inspired individuals. Somehow God filled a particular biblical spokesperson with unusual insight—which was at least partly captured in a biblical text. In this view, the text itself isn't fully inspired, but it witnesses, even if brokenly, to the original inspiration.[9]

"Salvation history" is another stance. Gnuse summarizes the approach of those who

> declare that God has acted decisively in the exodus and resurrection, that Scripture bears testimony to these events, and that the continued repetition of this salvific activity by God is rooted in the once and for all nature of these primal events.[10]

God inspires the events. Scripture is then a secondary record of those events, a step removed from them. It's important to us because it shares those events with us and stirs us to be shaped by them. But it isn't, itself, directly inspired.

Historicism

Timelessness yields to historicism. David Tracy says that "the primary task of modern interpreters is historical. . . . They are endeavoring to discover . . . what the texts and contexts they are interpreting meant to their authors in their relationships with their readers." Good interpreters must explore the historical setting in which authors and original readers functioned.[11]

This feature sharply distinguishes criticism from pre-criticism. An easy timelessness becomes unthinkable. One can't apply to the present Paul's words on female hair length and head covering without examining how Paul's historical setting shaped his thoughts. If something present in Paul's situation but not ours shaped Paul's views—maybe that only prostitutes cut their hair back then—those particular opinions may be irrelevant to us.

Similarly, some critics argue that the Bible's shapers knew nothing of loving, covenantal homosexuality. If so, antihomosexual biblical statements may not apply to such relationships. Even conservative thinkers do some historicist interpreting: witness the many Levitical prohibitions ignored today by most Christians.

Semi-closed universe

Historicism, combined with the scientific naturalism and rationalism that helped found critical thought, often creates for many critics a universe which is semi-closed at best. God isn't an all-powerful being who tears aside, at will, the curtain of scientific regularity. Instead, God works primarily within the regularities of nature science has identified. This closed understanding of what God is and isn't likely to do forces many critics to translate biblical accounts that seem to contain miracles into versions more comfortable to modern minds.

Miracles may be explained naturalistically. Or maybe they simply didn't happen and are merely figurative pictures of how God works. The Red Sea miracle becomes the nice reed sea coincidence—if it happened at all. Many critics don't fit the stereotype, but a few generations back some hardheaded critics would sooner have died than believe in a miracle.

If you *were* such a critic, reading that angels accompanied Jesus' birth, you might do a number of things. (a) You might try to understand the historical situation and mentality that made angels thinkable. (b) You might investigate whether angels are thinkable today and decide they're not, because scientific thinking makes such a notion laughable. (c) Therefore, you might conclude, angels are one part of the nativity story that's mostly meaningless to us or meaningful only as a symbolic picture.

Rationality

David Tracy points out that, until the last several generations, "critics laid great emphasis on the presumed objectivity of their studies."[12] They treated biblical criticism as a science involving the rigorous and logical analysis of data. When such rationalism is present in critical thought, interpretation through pious openness to the Spirit is unpopular. God speaks through source criticism, form criticism, redaction criticism, canonical criticism, criticism *ad nauseum*, not through subjective and irrational hunches or feelings.

Complexity
What I mean by complexity should be clear. The number of linguistic, historical, theological, philosophical, literary, and other disciplines the critic must master to interact properly with the Bible is mind-boggling. There is no hope for people in the pews. They truly are peons, forced to submit to the interpretation of whoever has the highest level of critical biblical literacy.

I don't mean to dismiss critical methodology. Complicated forces really *do* underlie the shaping of the Bible. We can't escape having our timeless and personal and subjective interactions with the Bible tested. Critical testing prevents our making the Bible a Rorschach inkblot onto which we project our fantasies—whether or not they have anything to do with the Bible's original meaning.

Mixed Authority
Criticism allows many understandings of authority. Some critics treat the Bible as a mostly human book with mostly low authority. Others treat it as a book which is humanly mediated but through which God can still speak. In this view, once criticism has identified God's voice speaking behind or through the human voices, what God says is, indeed, authoritative.

The bottom line is this: At least in theory (in practice the flesh of even precritics is weak) precritics are fully committed to the Bible's authority. Critics, in contrast, don't offer even theoretically firm authority. Each critic makes choices about each text's level of authority.

Critical Understandings of Tradition

Precritics gain relatively easy access to their traditions. Critics find distance gaping between them and their traditions. Several factors (related to the above discussion) cause the distance. They include: (a) Doubt that God spoke in more than broken ways to the all-too-human mediators of the tradition. (b) Awareness of the differences between historical eras. (c) Reducing causation and motivation to factors that can be discussed rationally. (d) A sense of the complexity of currents that shape traditions. This understandably weakens the tradition's authority over its adherents.

Mennonites are feeling some of this distancing. At midcentury a view of Anabaptism popularized by Harold S. Bender prevailed.[13] Bender's work was solid and scholarly but somewhat precritical. By the 1960s it was being challenged. Leonard Gross says that "everything and anything within Anabaptist history was now open to critique, with a number of scholars pushing hard to unseat, consciously, the work of earlier generations."[14]

Gross's words come from the foreword to a book by J. Denny Weaver, whose aim is to examine the many strands of tradition which formed early Anabaptism. This contrasts with Bender's approach, which assumed a simple beginning in Switzerland. The effect of a work like Weaver's is to make an appeal to the authority of Anabaptist tradition more difficult. *The* Anabaptist tradition (as opposed to many variations of it) may not exist.

Other traditions have been similarly affected. When Erik Erikson psychoanalyzed Martin Luther in *Young Man Luther*, he allowed some to see Luther as inspired more by private psychological demons than by God.

Here again authority is weakened. How can one sort out wisdom versus unbalanced emphasis caused, say, by unloving parents?

MARRYING CRITIC AND PRECRITIC

Why professors and students clash is hopefully coming clear. What to do about it is less clear. Is the answer for students and other precritics to rescue an apostate church from corrupt criticism? Or for professors to rescue precritics from dim-witted medieval obscurantism? Both positions simultaneously trouble and energize me. I've tried both myself. Neither, by itself, seems quite right. That has made me look for a better way. My tentative answer is imperfect, open to just criticism from both sides, but I propose it for whatever help it may offer fellow searchers.

Critics and precritics are like the hero and heroine of so many movies who hate each other's guts from the start. Movie rules being what they are, they are, of course, fated to endure many trials and tribulations in each other's warring company before falling in love. I believe they should marry, while retaining—as marriage partners should—separate identities. What might the marriage look like?

Paul Ricoeur offers important clues. If I understand him correctly, he suggests we can encounter in three ways the stories and symbols contained in a book like the Bible.[15] First is the precritical way. One might call it a first naïveté, an original innocence. We approach the Bible like children listening wide-eyed (before even they turn skeptical!) to a fairy tale. We don't probe and question. We let the tale of frogs who turn into princes and hags who turn into queens wrap us in its magic.

But as we grow we realize the fairy tale tells of things that don't ordinarily happen. We have to make a decision. We can suppress our new questions and choose fairy-tale reality over normal reality. Doing that may leave us with no way to address those hard realities of real life the tale knows nothing about.

We can, on the other hand, face the questions and see where they lead. Then we embark on a second way, the critical way. We lose our first naïveté. We now learn many important things about the tough, ordinary world through whose issues we have to thread our way every day. We learn many complicated and helpful things about the physiology of frogs and the psychological troubles of hags.

Oh, but what if, somehow, there's something true (even if sexist!) in tales of queens and princes? What if there's more to life than frogs and hags? If we wonder that, we open ourselves to the possibility of a second naïveté, a second innocence. This is the postcritical way. It appreciates precritical truths but hardens them, toughens them, makes them relevant to the modern world through critical testing.

Let me suggest specific features—aimed at the Bible but also pertinent to interaction with tradition—a postcritical marriage might have.

Direct Inspiration Mediated Through Humans

I don't want to ponder details of biblical inerrancy, infallibility, or reliability. I'll let others worry about that. I do want to affirm there's a way to capture the sound of God's music dancing through the Bible *and* the richness of the many human instruments which play the music. John R. W. Stott tries to articulate it. "The fundamentalist emphasizes so strongly the divine origin of Scripture that he tends to forget that it also had human authors who used sources, syntax and words to convey their message, whereas the evangelical remembers the double authorship of Scripture."[16]

There is tension, mystery, and paradox here, obviously. The temptation to simplify the matter by choosing only one alternative is strong. The creative choice is to hold both in tension. This means being open to God's music *and* doing the hard work needed to truly hear and appreciate it.

Timeless Historicism

Here the wedding creates what Noll calls "believing criticism." He argues that precriticism sometimes "treats the Bible as a magical book largely unrelated to the normal workings of the natural world."[17] God's transcendence is stressed at the expense of God's immanence, God's connection with everyday life.

Timelessness is an overemphasis on transcendence. At first glance it makes God very immediate, but it actually images God as skating over the surface of history. God's voice and actions thunder above those irrelevant historical settings and cultural contexts. God alights once in a while in an appropriate miracle but is hard to find in the humdrum little events making up most of history. That divorce of God from history is the danger of belief without criticism.

Criticism without belief, on the other hand, sees only history and hears no larger, timeless, transcendent voice.

When criticism joins with belief, however, God can speak through each historical situation while remaining larger than each situation. Timeless historicism, or believing criticism, owns a Bible in which God's voice speaks *within* historical situations and *through* and *beyond* the original situations to our current ones.

In this joining the two camps reveal and challenge each other's presuppositions. Critics can show precritics that what they often take to be God's timeless voice is actually a voice distorted by a subtly *deductive* approach (from general theory to specific application) to the Bible. Precritics, for example, may develop views about Jesus as personal Savior or being born again that owe their content to modern developments like tent revivalism. They may then read their views back into a Bible which doesn't always support them.

The critics' approach is *inductive* (from particular details to general principles). They try to read what's *really* in the Bible, not what theory says should be there. Precritics can show them that even this induction is easily clouded by questionable presuppositions —as when they rule out the possibility that Peter really walked on water.

Semiopen Universe

Because it helps me combine my mystical and romantic side with my hardheaded and critical side, this is my favorite area of marriage. Precritics are open to God's transcendence, God's power to do real, tangible work in the world.

Critics are cautious about this. They believe the Bible does sometimes need to be translated into modern understandings. Take the Bible's three-decker universe —heaven above, hell below, earth in the middle. Unless we want to rule out anything science can teach us, we know this and related notions aren't literally accurate. We know there's not a firmament which holds above us the waters of the sky. We know we can't find hell by drilling long and hard into the earth's crust.

If the Bible sees such things differently than we do, it may see other things differently, as well. Isn't it possible, for instance, that what the Bible calls casting out demons we might call psychological healing? Such critical sifting seems valid and needed to me. There's no point calling something by an old name if cultures have so shifted that we have a new name for the same thing.

But the point is only to identify what a particular text really meant or means, not to say that something genuinely miraculous can never have happened. This is where precritical openness comes in. Interestingly, this precritical insight is now gaining wider support. Grant notes the "decline in attempts to read the miraculous out of the original record. Miracle is deeply embedded in the gospel."[18] W. G. Pollard argues that science itself is changing and opening. It sees vistas of transcendence and mystery where once it saw only facts impermeable to the notion of God's action. "Science is . . . discovering that mystery is not so much a puzzle to be cleared up as an essential quality of reality by which what is known presents itself to us as strange, amazing and yet fascinating."[19]

I think it's possible to approach the Bible critically *and* remain open to the reality of storms strangely stilled and heavenly hosts announcing peace on earth. In a lovely book called *Walking on Water*, Madeleine L'Engle, author of fairy tales but fully aware of the issues posed by the modern age, says we can do anything Jesus, God incarnate, could do. She says that "in art we are once again able to do all the things we have forgotten; we are able to walk on water; we speak to the angels who call us; we move, unfettered, among the stars." Lest anyone think her comments are merely figurative, she later says, "Am I suggesting that we really ought to be able to walk on water? That there are (and not just in fantasies) easier and faster ways to travel than by jet or by car? Yes, I am."[20]

If Christianity ever recaptured this fairy-tale quality while keeping it critically disciplined, what a beautiful, alluring thing it would offer this aching world! It might then offer a true alternative to New Age and similar mentalities. They have arisen, I suspect, because the hunger for the transcendent, for fairy-tale elements of life which turn out to be true, is so hard to feed in modern Christianity.

62 / TRACKLESS WASTES AND STARS TO STEER BY

Simple Complexity

This feature of the marriage would recognize that the study of the Bible's origins and meanings poses complex questions. It would also recognize that what is going on in academia is problematic. I claim middle-brow intelligence and training at best, but I've had more chance than the average Christian to wrestle with academic issues. Many of them mystify me.

Structuralism and deconstructionism, for example, have much to offer. They're too much, however, for my small brain. I don't mean to say that those who understand such issues shouldn't study them. Their learnings will eventually trickle down to us lowbrows and probably help us. I do mean to say that we could use some reaiming of academic effort from chasing the latest nuances of the latest trend to figuring out how to talk to ordinary people.

There must be a way to recognize the complex issues but grapple with them in ways simple enough for the average person to follow. I'm at least trying to find it in this book.

Rational Piety

New respect for a way of gaining insight that required neither genius-level intellect nor rejected the fruits of intellect would aid simplification. I think rational piety offers that way. It *tests* hunches, intuitions, feelings, words from God sensed in times of prayer and meditation. It also remains *open* to them. When I prepare a sermon, I first read a text. I review critical commentaries. Then I let things germinate, somewhere down deep. Sometimes dreams come. Sometimes potent waking images. Sometimes strong feelings. I listen to them all.

Once I had to preach on Luke 11:1-13, which focuses on God's loving answers to prayer. I studied. I started writing. Nothing meaningful came. I listened some more and remembered a recent dream. Bad guys were chasing me—but I woke up to a sense of peace and safety. My dream connected with the text. I suspected I had my sermon. But first I went back to the commentaries and checked things more carefully. I tested whether my dream accurately captured the text's meaning. Deciding it did, I proceeded.[21] Other times, however, I've reluctantly discarded an image after testing it and finding it inapplicable. That's how rational piety works.

Flexible Authority

Flexible authority recognizes the need for some form of reliable authority. The fragmentary, somewhat optional form of authority offered by criticism is strengthened. This is needed. I doubt my forebears and other courageous Christians would have died as readily for their faith if faced with criticism's optional authority. The potential for rationalization would have been too seductive.

Criticism does, however, affirm a flexibility foreign to precriticism's often rigid authoritarianism. I'll say more about this in future chapters.

Making the Marriage Work: The Essential Role of Community

I should say something about the setting in which the above features of the marriage are worked out. Much of my discussion applies to individual Christians working out personal theologies to guide their interaction with biblical and traditional authority. Envisioning an additional setting enriches the discussion, however. I refer to the communal setting offered by the overlapping gatherings of congregations, denominations, and the worldwide Christian fellowship.

Community will crop up again later. What makes the communal setting important here is this: It allows individuals or small groups within their larger communities to be faithful to their own particular perspectives rather than conform to one uniform way of thinking and living. The individual or small group provides the passionately held perspective. The community blends the passions into a larger, more balanced whole.

I've offered a postcritical paradigm or lens that tries to blend the best of the precritical and critical paradigms. My hope is not, however, that everyone will agree I've found the best perspective and rush to adopt it. Such a hope would be unrealistic in any case.

I wish just one thing: that each group would value the other and offer similar grace to postcritics like me, whose calling is to work at a bridging synthesis.

Let me ponder a real-life example of how I wish this would work. There exists in the Mennonite Church a group of dissident, conservative Mennonites whose views might fit the precritical label. They call themselves the "Fellowship of Concerned Mennonites." Similar groups exist in other denominations. They want to guard the old ways, the old fundamentals, against the acids of criticism. On the other hand, a growing number of Mennonite academicians, students, pastors, and church leaders have been exposed to and are often committed to critical methodologies.

To no one's surprise, the two groups don't get along. An interesting example of this emerged when C. Norman Kraus, a professor perceived by precritics (perhaps unjustly) to belong to the critical camp, wrote a book on Christology.[22] George R. Brunk II, a leader of the Concerned Mennonites, wrote a pamphlet attacking Kraus's work.[23] Conferences were held, statements were made, thunder rolled.

Now the merits of each case don't concern me here nor am I competent to evaluate them. What does interest me is finding a way for the church to value the positive contributions of both. What often prevents this in such situations is each camp's need to prove the other wrong. What if each side simply granted that we need all parties to create a good marriage?

The precritics are keeping genuine truths alive. We need their insistence on a living, vibrant, fully inspired Bible whose divine author throbs with a majestic, wild power that truly can still storms, both on the Sea of Galilee and in our bullet-ridden cities.

We need the critics, who offer continually improving tools for understanding the biblical settings in which God's voice is embedded and through which it speaks.

We need the postcritics, who can value the best in both camps and try to bring them together.

It's a cliché, a truism, but still worth saying: We need each other. This is certainly true in my case, since my postcritical contribution depends on bringing insights developed by others into fruitful conversation. We can benefit from each other in community only as we each contribute our small piece to the whole.

Together, as we combine the insights of the old sacred home with the forces threatening, we can scratch a trail across the trackless wastes.

QUESTIONS FOR DISCUSSION AND REFLECTION

1. How do you think God does or doesn't speak in the Bible?
2. Do we live in an open or closed universe?
3. Is biblical interpretation simple or complex?
4. Is piety or reason more helpful to biblical interpretation?
5. What authority does the Bible have over your life? How does that authority function?
6. What authority does tradition have? How does that authority function?
7. Do you identify with the precritical, critical, or postcritical camps?

8. What are the strengths of each camp? What are their weaknesses?

9. What conflicts between camps have you experienced?

10. Is a community with space for all camps workable? Why or why not?

CHAPTER 3

Taking the World into the Bible

The preceding discussion of the Bible made one crucial assumption. The Bible—and faith grounded in it—matters. This is why we fuss about ways we might interact with it. Otherwise, why bother?

Is that, however, a valid assumption? Does the Bible matter? And if it does, how does it? Does it matter as the source of irreplaceable truth? Or merely as the source of picturesque symbols offering truth which, even if real, can also be found elsewhere? Those are some of the questions I now want to address. As I do so, I'll lean in the direction of the separatism described in Chapter One. Then in my next chapter I'll ask how translationism might add its enriching and complementary notes.

My growing valuation of separatism is rooted in personal experience. My formative years drummed into me the conviction that the Bible matters. If I rejected the Bible it would try to worm itself back into me even against my wishes. Because the Bible's importance is so ingrained in me, for many years I could afford the luxury of not worrying about its importance. I could take it for granted.

I took that luxury into my early years of pastoring. My passion was to make the Bible relevant. I'm sorry to utter such a tired old word as *relevant*, but it captures the truth of the matter. I had long felt imprisoned in a separatist bubble of thinking and living, an isolation chamber cutting me off from the life that really mattered—life outside.

Now I was far from home, far from the old churches, in a big sinful city, a pastor with some power to set the tone of things. Now I could proclaim my independence, step outside the bubble, and be free at last. I would do this by making the Bible relevant. This meant translating it into the ways of thinking and feeling within which I lived—the secular world's sociologies, psychologies, movies, TV shows, newspapers, newsmagazines, and books.

What I was doing was right, I believe. It was right for me and right for the many who were sharing with me the journey. It was right for the countless Christians who have gasped for fresh air in their own isolation chambers (more on that in my next chapter). Right though it was, however, I've since come to see it wasn't enough. To explain why, I need to talk about "plausibility structures."

PLAUSIBILITY STRUCTURES AND THE SOCIAL GROUNDING OF INDIVIDUAL PERSPECTIVES

Peter Berger begins the explanation. He says that a religious world will seem real to us only if it's adequately supported by an "appropriate plausibility structure."[1] Lesslie Newbigin clarifies Berger.

> Our sense of what is real is, to a large extent, a function of the society in which we live. It is almost impossible for an individual to deny steadily the reality of things that society regards as real, or to affirm the reality of things that society regards as illusions. The plausibility structures that largely control our perception of what is the case are socially produced.[2]

This means that what seems real and true and believable to us is determined by what the larger communities that shape us consider real, true, and believable. A community sees life through a certain grid, a certain set of spectacles, a certain paradigm or model of understanding—a "plausibility structure." It then teaches us to see life through that grid. Whatever doesn't quite fit the grid isn't fully real, true, believable.

Complex though this idea seems, we meet it first in grade school. We call it peer pressure. We worry so much about peer pressure because our sense of what's real or what's plausible can shift when we change peer groups. Someone who treasures premarital virginity, simple living, or pacifism may fall in with people who mock such values. In a few months, she or he may not even remember why the values were important in the first place. We're much less in control of our own belief and much more at the mercy of our peer groups than we think.

When I was making the Bible relevant, I was, without fully realizing it, surrendering to a peer group or plausibility structure different from the one which had taught me the Bible mattered. I was surrendering to a secular plausibility structure. This structure considers *self-actualization* (Maslow), *id* (Freud), or *semiautonomous complex* (Jung) meaningful. It considers *salvation, carnal nature,* or *demon* meaningless. Of course, I'm participating in that structure right now by using words like *plausibility structure*, which make me feel my comments will carry a certain scientific (or at least pseudoscientific) weight.

The problem with this approach is not that it translates, which is often justifiable, but that it spends capital that will be exhausted if not replaced. That capital is the assumption, remnant of a discarded separatism, that the Bible matters. How long can one spend that assumption, so to speak, before emptying the wallet?

How long can one use the Bible to prop up secular plausibility structures that are at least partly alien to it before the effort becomes pointless?

Not all that long, I think. When the secular structures call the shots and determine what really matters, the Bible soon fades. A poem replaces a psalm as call to worship. Movies, novels, popular songs—or Maslow, Freud, Jung—replace the text as the foundation for preaching. The venerable book is not to be seen in the pews. Let the poor old worn-out thing rest in peace.

Let me quickly say I'm not against any of those things *in their place*. But they have to know their place. And their place is to support, clarify, complement, enrich Scripture—not to replace it. When they do replace it, the church fades. Glenda Hope (speaking not in some enemy journal but *The Christian Century*, that noted outlet for liberal views) says that "the mainline Protestant church is in serious decline. Some go so far as to say it is dying."[3] Reasons for the decline are complex, but key among them is surely the relegation of the Bible, in mainline churches, to the sidelines. The Bible remains present but isn't seen as *the* source of truths available *only* in its pages.

The mainline experience exemplifies the dilemma that faces us when we translate our heritage away. The community to which most of us increasingly belong is the larger, nonbiblical world. That community no longer considers the Bible a plausible guide. We only consider plausible whatever that larger community considers plausible. Then how are we to prevent ourselves from replacing the Bible as authoritative guide?

The answer, I think, is that we won't. Having experimented with both having a Bible that mattered *and* being primarily a "worldly" person, a card-carrying member of our secular, homeless society, my current conclusion is that it doesn't work. You can't expect a notion from one plausibility structure to carry the same weight when you switch structures. That leaves you with several choices. I'll oversimplify and turn them into two starkly simple options: Either you abandon the Bible as primary guide or you dethrone the structures which prevent experiencing the Bible as plausible primary guide.

I'll turn shortly to a more extended discussion of a way we might dethrone structures which undercut the Bible. First let me explain why I'll focus on the Bible—instead of God, Jesus, the Holy Spirit, the church—as my main way of conceptualizing that into which we enter. I don't mean to yield to bibliolatry, to the worship of the Bible as idol. The Bible, as we often hear, isn't the object of our worship; it only reveals it. And that's precisely the point. If one enters the Bible, it finally reveals everything else one needs to know. This includes the journey toward God, through Jesus, under the power of the Spirit.

TAKING THE WORLD INTO THE BIBLE: THE THEORY

George Lindbeck and other scholars (Hans Frei, Paul Holmer, David Kelsey) form what is sometimes called the "New Yale Theology."[4] They offer a way to dethrone nonbiblical structures. They advocate a Christianity which resists taking the Bible into the world (translationism). It instead takes the world into the Bible (separatism).

Lindbeck works at this by inspecting various theories of religion and doctrine. He focuses on two. One, which has translationist tendencies, he calls experiential-expressive. This perspective sees religions as *expressing* inner *experience*. Religions are ways of translating "inner feelings, attitudes or existential orientations" into doctrines, symbols, or pictures that try to capture in tangible form what is ultimately inexpressible.[5] For example, when Christians speak of being born again, they're describing a mysterious inner transformation which any number of doctrines or pictures could capture. None would be exactly right, because the inner transformation is beyond exact description. But any doctrine or picture would at least point to some aspect of what it means to be born again.

This approach suggests there may be one basic set of inner experiences shared by all people, but many different ways of interpreting and expressing such experience. Various religious approaches represent various ways of understanding the one inner reality. Which approach people choose then becomes optional. What really count are "individual quests for personal meaning.... The structures of modernity press individuals to meet God first in the depths of their souls, and then, perhaps, if they find something personally congenial, to become part of a tradition or join a church."[6]

Those of us holding this perspective experience ourselves as independent individuals. We explore private depths which we think we own regardless of formative social influences.

We fool ourselves, thinks Lindbeck. We don't see that a *communal* plausibility structure teaches us to think we create ourselves *individually*.[7] The paradox, obviously, is that a cultural perspective fills us with that illusion. It's because the group shapes us to think the group doesn't shape us that we *think* the group doesn't shape us!

Lindbeck believes we need to turn the experiential-expressive theory upside down. We don't have changeless inner selves which religion helps us express. Instead, the religion by which we choose to live *shapes* a particular inner self. "Instead of deriving external features of a religion from inner experience, it is the inner experiences which are viewed as derivative."[8] We don't express ourselves through worship, for instance. Rather, worship expresses *us*. Lindbeck calls this perspective cultural-linguistic. While it isn't separatist in a naive, innocent, or precritical way, it affirms the separatist strategy of building a home distinct from the world.

The crucial feature of Lindbeck's model is that it doesn't take the Bible into the world; it takes the world into the Bible instead. Rather than translating the Bible's realities into the world's understandings, we see the world's realities from a biblical perspective.[9]

I hope by now the relation of this to my earlier discussion of spending up capital is becoming clear. Lindbeck is saying the reason Bible matters to me, and is woven into every fiber of my being, is that my upbringing shaped a self in which that was true. Eventually, if I sever my roots, a different inner self (shaped particularly by psychology, that language which most seduces me) will emerge. If that's the self I want, no problem. But if I want a Christian self, I'll need to get my self into a situation that shapes me differently.

Because I'm secular enough to want the rigorous reasoning Lindbeck offers, I've made much of his approach. Yet cultural-linguistics and plausibility structures are actually complicated ways of recovering a simple truth the Anabaptist/Mennonite tradition has always stressed. There are two kingdoms, two realms— God's and the world's. Our decision to pledge allegiance to one or the other will affect dramatically the shape of our souls.

Ways we might pledge allegiance to God's realm and promote God-shaped souls are my next concern.

TAKING THE WORLD INTO THE BIBLE: THE BUILDING BLOCKS

Biblical Orientation

The first building block of a biblically based house is probably self-evident. It's to affirm a stance toward Bible and world which makes the Bible the primary source and the larger world the secondary source of plausibility structures.

In theory, this is a basic separatist assumption. But is it really practiced? Conscious commitment to a biblical orientation asks even separatists to examine critically ways they may allow the larger world to set the agenda. Many U.S. separatists, quick to sense innate Republican conservatism, are Republicans. Are they shaped by biblical or Republican agenda? Do those who sell a gospel of wealth, power, and success worship the biblical God or a seductive Mammon called the free-enterprise system?

A biblical orientation asks even more of translationists. They must critically evaluate not only practice (perhaps as Democrats!), but basic theory. The Bible calls the translationist to repentance, to a radical turnabout in loyalties. What a radical reversal of liberal mainline decline such a turnabout might produce! Maslow, Jung, Freud, and all the other "isms" and "ologies" to which translationists have sold their souls could give way to Jesus.

Now I don't want to back myself into a corner here. As I keep warning, I'm headed toward praise of translationism. What I mean by labeling the Bible primary is that it sets the tone, shapes the discussion, takes precedence. Making translationism secondary doesn't negate its importance. My marriage is my primary nuclear family relationship. It must remain strong so I can properly nurture my secondary relationships with my children. Yet with my children still young and needy, I probably spend more actual time and energy on them than on my spouse. Translationism is in much the same place my children are in my priorities: secondary but crucial.

Biblically Oriented Community

The second building block is biblically oriented community. Both the notion of plausibility structures and Lindbeck's cultural-linguistic approach demand this. That's because both assume that social and communal forces inevitably shape individuals. They must be nurtured in a particular community to develop a particular individual identity.

Under the onslaught of secular individualism we may be forgetting another truth Mennonites have long understood: We don't pledge allegiance to God's realm as isolated individuals. We do so in community, promising to support each other on a journey no one can make alone.

Biblically oriented community exists at many levels, from the worldwide Christian fellowship down through denominations to congregations. Much of the action, however, happens at the congregational level. This is where, if anywhere, we create a peer group strong enough to challenge other mentalities. Larger communities, including Christian media and schools, may support our project. But it's in the congregation that we weave or unravel the complex tapestry of thinking and behaving and feeling in biblical categories. So important is the congregation that I'll examine the remaining building blocks within that context.

Biblically Oriented Leadership

Congregations wanting to build a biblical house need biblically oriented leadership. They need women and men who pastor, preach, teach, and counsel with a clear commitment to take the world into the Bible and not the Bible into the world. Finding such people isn't easy. People who ignore the larger world need not apply. Wanted are those blessed with deep and sophisticated understanding of the larger world who work at translating its understandings and insights back into biblical categories.

Such people might examine an American election,

for example, and do more than evaluate in conventional terms whether the Democrat or Republican is better. They might turn to the biblical prophets' analysis of wealth and poverty and God's interaction with such issues. Then they might judge the politicians within this framework.

Translating the world back into biblical understandings is particularly tricky when counseling. Both Christians and non-Christians offer plenty of sound therapy that simply brackets the question of how therapeutic issues relate to the Bible. That's valid. There are issues people need to struggle with which the Bible simply doesn't address. More troubling is counseling which operates in a realm entirely different from the Bible's, meaning that never the two shall meet—or even that they work against each other.

Congregations need people who tie what goes on in counseling back to the larger biblical framework. There are spiritual directors (sometimes pastors) who understand psychological language but see life as a journey toward God, rather than toward whatever state a particularly theory considers wholeness. They can build helpful bridges. Neill Q. Hamilton exemplifies this. Though aware of and indebted to basically secular theories of moral and faith development proposed by James Fowler and others, he reshapes them to fit a biblical framework. Stages with names like "discipleship phase," "the cross as the end of illusion," "transition to life in the Spirit" are the result.[10]

Biblical Language

Biblically oriented congregational leaders and participants keep biblical language in their liturgy, preaching, worship, sharing of ordinances, and common life together. This doesn't mean sticking with King James or insisting on archaic words whose "biblical" sound owes more to Elizabethan England than to the Bible itself. It *does* mean refusing to replace biblical terms and concepts entirely with nonbiblical or, as Lindbeck puts it, "extratextual" ones. It means learning what the New Yale Theologians often call the "grammar of the faith." Let me look at several related examples of how this might work.

The biblical word *sin* could be translated into the extratextual word *maladjustment*. There might be some justification for that. Sin contributes to maladjustment. But when maladjustment entirely replaces sin, the power of the biblical word to set the agenda is lost. Discussion gradually moves further and further from biblical roots.

Maladjustment implies that a twist of a screw, a shift in the psychic carburetor setting, will make the motor hum. A little rich on id, a little lean on ego. "Please, Mr./Ms. Psychotherapeutic Mechanic, adjust my engine!" This weakens our understanding of sin as basic transgression against God's purposes. It encourages a therapy-shaped machine at the expense of a God-shaped soul.

The biblical word *grace* is often translated into the extratextual *unconditional acceptance*. God unconditionally accepts me. No matter what I do, God loves me. There is truth to that. Truth, and a clarity that grace, an alien term, doesn't offer. I discovered this when a woman just getting used to biblical language said she had always thought grace meant the quality you observe when a dog moves gracefully across the floor. The problem is that unconditional acceptance often turns into a shallow tolerance. You do your thing, I'll do mine. Sometimes we'll mess up, but God will still tolerate us and think we're okay.

How much more richness grace can offer—grace carefully interpreted and connected to the modern mind, but resolutely retained. Grace says I sin, I violate myself and reality in ways more basic and complex than *maladjustment* can ever capture. Still there is hope. God "forgives" me. (*Forgive* is another potent word usable only if one keeps sin and grace.) God restores me to good and joyful relationship with all creation and its Creator.

I had the choice once, when talking to a divorced friend whose marriage had been messy, of absolving his guilt by saying the messiness didn't matter. I could just accept it. Or I could say (as I did) that the messiness *did* matter. He *had* sinned. Yet still I loved him. Still I believed in the integrity that would deepen in him as he faced, "repented" of (also meaningful only in a sin/grace/forgiveness framework), and made amends for his sin. The first approach is banal and stirs no change. The second offers rich meaning and a call to new life.

Strong Doctrinal Identity

One way to hold onto a solid core of key biblical understandings is to develop a strong doctrinal identity. Doctrinal affirmations can range from broad ecumenical statements of faith to specific statements of congregational belief, but their underlying purpose is the same. It's to create a simple and sharply focused summary of biblical understandings strongly held by a community.

As helpful as doctrinal statements are, however, their power to reach the whole person is limited. They easily become dry, bloodless, point-by-point outlines. These reach that small part of the brain which takes tests and writes term papers. They miss the large part of our beings that sings and weeps, moans and exults at a level no doctrinal statement can reach. How can we address that level? How can we wrap our whole beings in the realities the Bible reveals?

Story

The answer is *story*. Story is a crucial way much of

the foregoing comes alive, becomes flesh, is incarnated in the often messy real lives of real people living in the real world. We can wrap congregational participants in a different master story than the master stories they're living out. This is another simple way of talking of plausibility structures.

I stress story because I, along with many others these days, think we're profoundly shaped by stories. This fashionable focus on story is a fad which, like all fads, will soon fade. But I think some truths will survive. The trend emerged because we needed it. An overly propositional style had imprisoned Christian conversation. Somehow the notion had arisen that one can best capture faith stances through propositions, through factual and logical statements.

This isn't an entirely mistaken view, as my comments on doctrine indicate. Genuine and helpful exchange of information happens that way, but the real power lies in stories. This is because propositions are secondary to stories. They are summaries of the truths throbbing more fully and vibrantly in stories.

Charles V. Gerkin says that "choices and decisions are . . . informed more fundamentally by levels of human experience that are at their deepest level metaphorical—that is, imagistic, symbolic, and affective—rather than by reason."[11] Stories are vital because they speak to the side of us that responds to imagery and is rooted in feelings. Gerkin considers that part of us to be the one which most deeply shapes us.

Propositions, on the other hand, speak more directly to our intellects, which are important but hold less power to shape us. June Alliman Yoder says this:

Take the proposition, "Love your neighbor." . . . I don't quite understand what it means to love my neighbor until I can take it apart in the story of the good Samaritan. We can *see* stories in a way that we can't in a propositional statement. We can see stories in our mind, and in my mind's eye, I see the story of the good Samaritan taking place on a winding road that's between Wayland and Washington, Iowa.[12]

I know this is all arguable, but let me give some storylike examples to buttress my point instead of engaging in extensive rational argument.

My own life experience certainly justifies to me the importance of story. What has shaped me, to the extent any of us can be conscious of what shapes us, is story more than proposition. My Christian self was most deeply shaped by a mingling of biblical stories, the life stories of those important to me, and stories I met in countless books. Propositions saying "God is this," or "The Christian life follows x, y, z rules" haven't been irrelevant, but they *have* been secondary to the stories.

Christianity didn't really touch my depths until I met it as naked story, in the form of C. S. Lewis's *Chronicles of Narnia*. I may be a grown-up, trying here, at least, to write grown-up truth. Behind my grown-up faith, however, I owe quite a debt to those books for children. A wondrous lion bounds into the story to sing a world into being. Later he warms that beloved land of Narnia after the White Witch freezes it. Then he dies. I can never experience Good Friday and Easter without remembering Susan's and Lucy's tears for dead Aslan, and then their joy as they ride risen Aslan's back and cling to his lion's mane.

I do sometimes wish I could disentangle Lewis a bit from my faith, because he had his flaws. But the very difficulty of doing that witnesses to the power of story. Propositional clarification of Lewis's deficiencies is no match for the grand wild sweep of his stories.

Nor is the dry recitation of doctrinal positions any match for a culture which communicates its plausibility structures most powerfully through stories and images —thrown at us particularly by TV, MTV, movies. Oh, you get the occasional Bill Moyers documentary and the occasional TV commercial which makes a propositional claim, and these can be good and effective ways to communicate. What really makes things throb, though, are those images and pictures strung together to tell stories. Even Bill Moyers communicates most powerfully through stories—as in "The Power of Myth," his PBS interviews with Joseph Campbell, that great student and teller of stories.

Tell me I should be an idealist willing to fight corruption in government. I yawn. Show me Frank Capra's classic tale of an innocent senator fighting Washington's corruption in *Mr. Smith Goes to Washington*. Corny the movie may be, but it tempts me to take the first AMTRAK train to Washington and talk to some senators myself.

Tell me I should be a sacrificial person. Boredom glazes my eyes. My soul runs from your demand. Tell me about a man who danced toward Jerusalem, through all opposition, even as his heart broke and his life bled away. Explain to me the connections between his story and my story, which doesn't seem to go right when I make avoiding sacrifice the idol my culture makes it. Something within me comes to life. New life beckons. My story enters Jesus' story, and together we dance through pain toward joy and new life.

I've focused so far on the simple fact that stories are worth using because they're so powerful. Another reason stories are crucial to taking the world into the Bible is that the Bible *is* story. It's like a fat, complex novel, only there are those of us who claim the story the novel tells is finally true. And many of the texts presented within that overarching, novel-like structure are themselves story or storylike—history, biography, poetry, gospel narrative.

Stanley Hauerwas says that "Christian convictions take the form of a story, or perhaps better, a set of stories that constitutes a tradition, which in turn creates and forms a community." He adds that Christian ethics (another way of talking about the soul-shaping project) "does not begin by emphasizing rules or principles, but by calling our attention to a narrative that tells of God's dealing with creation."[13] So to enter the Bible *is* to enter an inexhaustible supply of stories—stories unfolding within the Bible's master story and its movement from creation and fall through redemption to consummation.

Great movies shape us by stirring our identification with grand (though flawed) characters undergoing thrilling adventures and in some way changing the world. Sir Richard Attenborough's *Gandhi*, for example, lingers in both conscious thought and unconscious depths. It calls its viewers to let Gandhi's life shape theirs.

The Bible, properly entered as stirring narrative, holds such power. It could change sermons, worship hours, and devotional times from the bland things they often are into spine-tingling events shaking drowsy souls into vibrant life.

When the Bible's master story comes alive, it makes secular master stories seem thin and pale. We're random collections of molecules which developed from a random process set in motion by a chance explosion that began the universe, says one secular story. Our souls shrivel. Why bother with living? Why not pursue happiness as highest goal?

There is truth, certainly, in scientific views of life's development. Tell us, however, about how God brooded over the face of the deep, and then called us forth to share in the tale God is telling through an unfolding creation. Tell us that, and our souls glow with purpose and meaning. Nobody knows the troubles we've seen, we may sing. But God does, and God will redeem all troubles, seen and unseen.

RESULTS OF TAKING THE WORLD INTO THE BIBLE

Three possible results of taking the world into the Bible deserve additional comment. They are reversal, a community of outcasts, and biblical politics.

Reversal

Running through the Bible is the principle of *reversal*.[14] The Israelites, that motley band of nomadic sinners chosen by God to spread light to all nations, exemplify it. When they say God sides with poor widows against oppressive rulers, the prophets utter it. Jesus, world's Savior but born in a stable, victorious precisely when defeated, most clearly lives it out. Reversal says God's ways are surprising, topsy-turvy, different from the world's. It says if we think we've got it made, we'd better look out. And if we know we'll never make it, why, God be praised, that's exactly when we will!

When we enter the Bible, we don't just take life as usual into it and allow the good book to baptize the status quo. The Bible throws reversal at any efforts to do that. When we use all tools for letting the Bible truly speak, including precritical, critical, and postcritical ones, the Bible challenges old notions and calls for new life.

A Community of Outcasts

Challenges to the community's worn-out ways must be more than theoretical, however. The idea of plausibility structures suggests the community's *social* structures must change for new insight to prevail. A community which wants to believe in reversal will have to provide a setting in which reversal is, in fact, believable. It will need members whose presence creates new plausibility structures supporting the plausibility of reversal. It will have to welcome those who deeply know what it means to be touched by reversal. It will have to bring outcasts into its midst—those who don't fit the dominant plausibility structures.

This means women, with *all* their gifts. People of different races. The homeless, poor, unwashed. Those rejected by traditional orthodoxies, including the agnostic searchers such as I once was and partly remain. Sinners who smoke and drink, who've had divorces and abortions and affairs. Homosexuals.

I don't mean by this that we condone sin or consider disciplined living irrelevant. Not at all. Any sinner needs redemption. I simply mean that such people know the meaning of losing, of exclusion, of reversal. They therefore force us to see the Bible in ways that are true to the biblical story and its upside-down themes. This fits with liberation theology's argument that poor and outcast and oppressed people can enter the Bible more quickly than wealthy and successful people. This is because their life experience is closer to the experience of those whose salvation stories the Bible celebrates.

As a preacher trying to sense the mood, spirit, and needs of a congregation, I try to be conscious of the way the community shapes me. This has helped me see the importance of outcasts. When I sense my audience consists of powerful, influential people, I'm tempted to preach a gospel which empowers us to help others. I'm tempted to become a powerful person preaching to other powerful people about ways we can use our power for good. This isn't all bad. When we have power we need to acknowledge it and use it for good ends. But it's dangerous because it fosters the illusion that we who are powerful control our destinies, the destinies of others, and even the next chapter of God's story.

When, on the other hand, I sense losers in my audience, I try to touch the loser in myself. I'm stirred to ask God—and not my own limited, egotistic resources—to empower and guide me. My preaching then reflects that. We empowered losers, filled with God and not illusory self-importance, are likely to make a bigger difference than all the world's hotshots. That's why we so desperately need outcasts, experts in reversal, among us. We need them to help us all shape a peer group that truly believes losing in the world can be a way of winning for God.

Biblical Politics

Volumes are written on Christians and politics. I can't hope to encompass the important issues here. I simply want to make one central point rooted in William H. Willimon and Robert L. Wilson's discussion of the United Methodist Church's decline and strategies for revitalization. They suggest the UMC has confused "its peculiarly Christian values with the dominant values of American culture." Then when the UMC takes political stands, it has no unique source of insight in which to root them. The result is unmoored political activism which simply makes the church one more interest group, one more lobbying faction in the political arena.[15]

The authors aren't against political stands *when* they flow from the church's "own worship and mission, which is expressed through its life in society. The relation of the church to society is one in which the worship of God sends one out in service."[16] The point is that the church's first priority, once again, is to enter into the Bible, and allow it to do its shaping. The church can then, out of that shaping, take the Bible's implications back out into the world.

Stanley Hauerwas holds a similar view. He sees the world as dependent on structures, powers, and institutions whose false foundation is "shared resentments and fears." The church's power to transform lies in offering the world an alternative: "Jesus is the story that forms the church. This means that the church first serves the world by helping the world to know what it means to be the world."[17] The church gives the world a baseline against which to measure itself by trying to live on the true foundation of God through Jesus.

The world, for instance, often rightly calls for an inclusive, unified planet. Paradoxically, Christians help that happen by rooting themselves deeply in their own particular story. Its plot then sends them back out into the world "to break down arbitrary and false boundaries between people." Christians do this as disciples of Jesus, a stronger, more enduring motivator than "facile doctrines of tolerance or equality."[18]

This approach doesn't offer neat answers to questions of political stance and strategy. It does call the church to a style of political thinking that sets its own agenda over society's agenda. This will sometimes include accepting (with Jesus) faithful defeat rather than compromised victory

• • •

In this chapter I am indeed affirming much of what fundamentalists, sectarians, conservative evangelicals, traditional Mennonites, and others are already doing. I'm affirming all who see the church as called to build deviant, nonconformed, alternative plausibility structures.

But no matter how much I affirm an old separatism or plead for a renewed one, the competing forces remain strong. Even such well-practiced deviants as Mennonites no longer want to pay the price associated with deviance. We reject the odd, quaint, meaningless loser status the dominant structures try to impose on us. The many versions of separatism which have been and continue to be tried are mostly no match for the forces of modernity.

I have little hope that the vision I've sketched will,

by itself, be enough to revitalize the church. It provides building blocks, yes. But we also need mortar. Translationism (and its friendship with the modern age) offers the mortar. We need a separatism which incorporates the modern age, not merely defends against it. Os Guinness, in a book purporting to offer reports from a "Central Security Council" determined to destroy Christianity, says that

> the worst thing that could happen is this: The increasingly apparent weakness and captivity of the church might jolt Christians into seeing the force of the extremes and then spur a movement to recover a coherent and balanced, ruthlessly biblical, "third way." If you like, a resistance movement content to be neither *emigres* nor collaborators. The time for such a movement is ripe, for if the sixties illustrated the absurdities of extreme liberalism, the late seventies has done the same for extreme conservatism. The cry "A plague on both your houses!" would be a fitting tribute to our work, but it could also spell trouble for us. Nostalgia for a golden age is harmless, the desire for a golden mean is not.[19]

I want to turn next to a quest for that golden mean, asking how translationism, added to separatism, might create a radically different Christianity—one truly not of the world while remaining thoroughly in it.

QUESTIONS FOR DISCUSSION AND REFLECTION

1. Does the Bible matter? Why or why not?
2. Do you agree that particular peer groups and the plausibility structures that shape them create or color our perceptions of truth?
3. Are you or is your congregation in danger of spending its capital of biblical faith and formation? If so, how?
4. Can we maintain our Christian beliefs by our-

selves? Or only in Christian community, as the concept of plausibility structures suggests?

5. Does your church primarily take the Bible into the world or the world into the Bible?

6. What changes might take place in your church if "taking the world into the Bible" became a priority?

7. Are stories or statements of fact more important to you?

8. Do you agree or disagree that you need to be careful what kind of community your church is because that will determine what truths you hold dear?

9. Should a church be a "community of outcasts"?

10. What do *your* "biblical politics" look like?

CHAPTER 4

Connecting Bible and World

My goal for this chapter is hard to meet but easy to state. It's to show the virtues of translationism's attempt to value the modern world. I want to show that a home big enough and strong enough to take the world into the Bible needs the larger world's truths as mortar. I'll maintain the priority of separatism established in the previous chapter but will affirm translationism's longing to make the Bible meaningful in our world.

Valuing the translationist urge to connect Bible and world is crucial. This is because those separatist homes built solely on traditional, conservative, reactionary, or escapist strategies are too brittle to survive secular storms. They don't really take the world into the Bible. At their worst, they take themselves out of the world into a home which seems biblical but is only a museum preserving a dead past. How do we take a living world into a living Bible?

BUILDING A CRITICAL
AND SELF-CONSCIOUS FOUNDATION

The first way is implicit in the preceding chapter. I affirm separatist strategies, but I do so—and this is key—in a critical and self-conscious way. I don't simply return to an innocent, precritical, premodern Eden. Instead (to the limited extent I understand them), I accept the realities of the modern world. I then try to build a home on a foundation that accepts those realities.

Such a strategy recognizes there's no returning to an era untainted by pluralism, relativism, loss of authority, and so on. Those chasing the chimera of a return simply consider their way right, authorized and legitimated by God, and other ways wrong. My approach assumes there's no knowing, in the old secure and unquestioning way, that our way, the Christian way, is *the* right way.

If we take seriously the notion of plausibility structures, and face its implications squarely, we're left with an unsettling realization. We have no foolproof way of absolutely knowing our way is the true way. This is because we can't fully pierce the curtain of plausibility structures that shape our views of truth to see the naked reality behind them. We always see, as our good apostle Paul realized, as if through a glass, darkly.

Someone like me, whose plausibility structures were shaped by an odd mix of fundamentalist Mennonite and secular, white middle-class influences, will always see truth through a glass darkened in a particular way. I'll never know precisely what truth I would see if I had grown up, say, in a passionately Hindu Indian home. Or a secular humanist liberal American home whose members considered fundamentalists to be kooks. Or the home of poor Hispanic migrant workers.

I'm aware that some thinkers try to find universal truths convincing to all, no matter what contexts or peer groups have shaped them. Then they try to build on this sure foundation a Christianity whose claims to truth are universally compelling. Arthur F. Holmes, appropriately, calls this "foundationalism"[1] Such strategies don't convince me. Our many allegiances to many different truths suggest that no way of making one truth compelling to all has been found.

They also assume that logical, rational, and philosophical argument can provide convincing reasons for judging one truth claim truer than another. Such argument doesn't persuade me. It's unlikely to persuade most people, who (like me) understand only the merest shadow of what one has to master to make truth judgments in that way.

At the level of theoretical, intellectual argumentation, we probably *are* reduced to (or blessed by!) pluralistic thinking. We need to accept the possibility of many truths. And we need to recognize that the truths which strike us as truest are those our peer groups and their plausibility structures shape us to experience as most compelling. Christianity can't plead exemption from this modern understanding.

But here's the crucial thing about a Christianity that accepts this admittedly slippery foundation. It can remind those who cling to other truths that their foundation, being the same one, is *equally* slippery. Though secular insight, for example, will feel most compelling to a person shaped by secular plausibility structures, it's no better grounded than Christian insight.

The discussion can then shift from intellectual argument to asking a more profound question. (Only geniuses can conduct arguments according to rules academic plausibility structures consider valid anyway.) Which home, created by which plausibility structure, offers the most warmth, love, and satisfaction? To put it at a level even our inner child (who makes our deepest decisions) can understand, which home feels most like home?

That approach, though modern, is not alien to good old-time Christianity or the simple theology which has sustained traditional Mennonites. Does Jesus establish his truths by engaging his disciples in complex philosophical argument? No! "Follow me!" he says. "Each tree is known by its own fruit," he says. Jesus asks not how well you can argue but how well you can follow. And he says that if you, along with fellow pilgrims, do follow, you'll be entrusting yourself to an odd new plausibility structure that will bear fruit. It will give you a Jesus shape.

In academic terms, you can't prove this shape is more valid than the Madison Avenue shape offered you by one of the world's alternatives to Jesus. But in your heart, in your soul, in your deepest being, you sense you might die for a Jesus shape—never for a Madison Avenue shape. Madison Avenue thinks that's a crazy perspective. This is what you'd expect. Jesus' way is always foolish in the world's eyes. It can never be justified in the world's language.

I've stumbled, I know, into that agelong debate over whether understanding seeks faith or faith seeks understanding. Clearly I support the latter—but not in an anti-intellectual way. Not in, as Holmes puts it, a "fideistic" way which "stakes its truth-claims directly and uncritically on what is believed." I lean toward what Holmes labels "coherentism." This describes justifying a belief "by virtue of its coherence within the entire body of what one knows and believes."

This remains a faith-seeking-understanding stance, because our worldviews, our guiding perspectives, do "arise at the prephilosophical level, in the whole-personal context of human existence and reflection."[2]

Though this stance is rooted in faith, it still values critical, rational judgment, however. We need such judgment to sift the wheat from the chaff when a myriad truths press their claims. My stance certainly uses intellect at least to show that starting from the same base as any other truth doesn't make defending Christianity impossible. And to show that we can accept modern questions and our inability to *prove* that any particular truth is true—and still be passionate Christians.

A separatist house built on this foundation of critical, self-conscious choice to be Christian (while knowing we could make other choices which would make other ways seem true) is a house which can stand storms. Like a skyscraper, it can flex in the wind, rather than stand rigidly against the gale until it breaks. When we live in this house we can cheerfully and nondefensively admit we can't prove our truth, even as we remain committed to our particular house. We all have to choose our house, or have a house choose us if we refuse conscious choice. So why not choose this one? If it's a good house, it will confirm itself. It will be solidly coherent. If it's a bad one, we can always leave.

BUILDING TRANSLATIONIST BRIDGES BETWEEN BIBLE AND WORLD

A second way we connect a living Bible with a living world is by seeing that the urge to translate, though easily misused, has a legitimate source. It flows from the recognition that a gap does exist between the Bible and the contemporary world. We *are* shaped by contemporary plausibility structures—in ways so potent we can never be more than dimly conscious of them. We must build bridges spanning the gap between the Bible and those structures.

Though we're probably more conscious of this gap than the ancients were, the gap isn't exclusively a modern phenomenon. We see it in the Bible itself. There have always been gaps between God's story and particular expressions of it. We have always needed ways to bridge the gap.

The New Testament abounds with evidence of bridge-building, particularly between the good news about a Jewish Jesus and Greek culture. John's Gospel, for example, refuses to translate the Jewish Jesus away even as it speaks to selves created by gnostic plausibility structures. The Old Testament offers similar evidence. Take the Genesis creation stories. They show traces of interaction with other creation stories even as they hold firm to their own understanding of God's creative work.

We need similar bridges between the Bible and selves created by nonbiblical structures before we can see the Bible as important and want to enter its world. Suppose I'm a dog. Suppose you tell me the Bible is a book full of stories about elephants and the way the Elephant God interacts with them. I'll assume this elephant Bible can't address my persistent self-destructive urge to dig a hole under my fence, run away, and become a miserable stray, fated to starve or die by SPCA injection. If I'm to take the Bible seriously, you need to show me connections between the specific elephant situations the Bible addresses and my life as a dog.

There are countless ways of building bridges between Bible and world. It's said Karl Barth used to urge reading the Bible with one hand and the newspaper with the other. Anyone who takes seriously the Bible's world *and* the contemporary world is constantly, both consciously and unconsciously, building bridges. Let me turn now to some examples of bridge-building.

Systemic Thinking in Sociology and Family Systems Theory

There is in the Old Testament understanding of people a notion about corporate personality or communal solidarity. It's expressed in the story of Achan, whose personal sin stained the entire tribe and required that he and all his family be stoned.[3] Here's a biblical concept that once made no sense to my thoroughly individualistic worldview. It seemed outmoded savagery.

There *is* savagery in Achan's stoning that I don't want to translate into the present. But corporate personality has come alive for me through the many current rediscoveries of the social links which shape us and bind us together, however much we may deny them.

Plausibility structures are *sociology's* way of helping us see ourselves as deeply dependent on our social context.

Family systems theorists are stressing that we're profoundly shaped by both our present families and by legacies handed down through many generations.

There are deep, sad rifts running through both sides of my personal family tree as well as my larger Mennonite family. One reason I'm writing this book, and writing from a stance that tries to bridge traditional and modern perspectives, is that I feel a passion to heal such rifts. An uncle, who no doubt inherited it from a previous generation, handed down to me the legacy of "bridger," "healer," "diplomat," and stirred my passion.

These *systemic* ways of thinking help us recover a contemporary understanding of the ties that bind. They also help us see meaning in a biblical concept that might once have seemed irrelevant.

Bridging Bible and Experiential-Expressivism

I experienced a rift between the Bible and my modern self that made me reject biblical faith for many years. I knew there was something about who I was—though I wasn't sure what—that the Bible didn't address.

George Lindbeck has helped me understand what was going on. He talks about that dominant Western way of understanding religion and our lives in the world, "experiential-expressivism." Lindbeck notes that those of us shaped by this tradition see religion as springing from something deep within us. We then express this *something* in outer rituals.[4]

Thus the location of important religious transactions

moves down into our depths. This is a dramatic change from the image which used to hold, of a relationship between humans down here on earth and God up or out there in heaven. Examining that change was John A. T. Robinson's project in *Honest to God*.

Other cultural factors have made a God "out there" more difficult to visualize. When we went into space we realized God wasn't literally out there, so where was God? Inside us, came the answer for many. Sigmund Freud, C. G. Jung, and others came to believe that within us there exist unconscious depths. They thought religious feeling sprang from this unconscious side of us. Such depth psychologies helped intensify our Western experience of reality as unfolding within us, rather than between us and a God out there.

Even as I grew up within my fundamentalist Mennonite home, I was paying keen attention to the world around me. School, books, and the news media particularly influenced me. I was being shaped by structures that assumed the importance of the self inside me. That, I believe, is why I never got very far trying to relate to a God out there, some being sitting far away whose attention I tried to lasso through prayer.

The breakthrough which pulled me back into Christianity was reconceiving God as down "in here," deep inside me. I then saw God as the reality I most fully touched in moments when the mystery and magic of life seemed to blossom joyously within. That bridge, that image of God as within which made sense to my experiential-expressivist self, was crucial to my reentry into the Bible.

New Age spirituality has arisen, I suspect, precisely to meet the needs of souls shaped by experiential-expressivism. Imaging God as within builds a bridge between the Bible and New Age thought. Deeply attracted to a God within, New Age adherents often visualize us as having divine inner essences whose release and expression make us into new, whole beings.

Caution is due here. I'm not advocating craven submission to our modern need to image God as within. As I've gradually come to see myself as taking the world into the Bible rather than the Bible into the world, I've seen that imaging God as within can be dangerous. When we worship a God inside us, our image can easily collapse into equating God and self. We translate God into self. In effect we create our own idolatrous god.

My journey back into the Bible is prompting me to critique the limits of the God-within image. It's helping me recapture the biblical insistence on a Creator who, however imaged, is always larger than, always transcends, the creature. But turning to a God within was a necessary stage in my journey toward the God of the Bible.

PSYCHOLOGY AS SOURCE OF ENLIVENING PERSPECTIVES

Another related way of imaging taking a living world into a living Bible is to see the world's truths as helping a once-dead Bible and the dead traditions rooted in it live again. To put it simply, when we open the windows of a stifling separatist home to the world, fresh air can blow in. This openness to the world's truth is rooted in the assumption that God created the world, the whole world. All truth we find in it is God's truth. Sin clouds that truth, which is why we have to work so hard to let the Bible test truth. But sin doesn't fully eradicate the truth still weaving its way through a flawed but good creation.

There are many sources of fresh air. I'll focus on psychology, not necessarily because it's the best source but because it has been particularly helpful to me and could be to others whose journey has paralleled mine.

Before going on to critique psychology's limitations, Charles V. Gerkin pauses to affirm it.

> Because of the careful and sensitive work of pastors informed by psychology, countless persons have achieved liberation from moralistic conscience, inappropriate dependence upon parental authorities, the demands of oppressive expectations of others.

Gerkin adds that psychology can offer healing when problems are caused by "ills that block self-realization."[5]

Four Ills, Four Antidotes

Gerkin lists three ills psychology can heal. These ills are fostered particularly, I believe, by separatism. I want to add a fourth—repressing evil—and pair each with psychology's antidote. I'll be hopelessly mixing psychological theories purists would keep discrete.

Moralistic Conscience, Unconditional Acceptance

Separatists know right and wrong. We know from the Bible, our preachers, our parents, our writers determined to exorcise the merest hint of the color gray, what's what in the morality business. We easily fill each other with prickly, picky tender moralistic consciences that fear grave sin has been committed if someone yells, "Shut up!" or sneaks a peak at the *Sports Illustrated* swimwear issue.

Such a conscience can rob you of all freedom, all joy, all ability to take creative risks. It can fill you with the underlying conviction that you are fundamentally a bad person no matter how passionately you throw yourself on Jesus' saving blood. This I've often seen, both in myself and the many people from such backgrounds I've counseled as pastor.

Imagine then what happens when such a person, feeling bound and gagged in an airless box, meets for the first time a central counseling tenet: unconditional acceptance. Even therapists have some disclosure responsibilities if told of things that involve harming another, but they don't judge most of what they hear. They listen to it carefully, sensitively, openly. There is now therefore no condemnation in the therapist's office, one could say. And that's often where people suffering from moralistic conscience first truly experience what it means to suffer no condemnation.

In such a setting, a person can face what Christians often pretend isn't true: *All* have sinned and fallen short of the glory of God. They continue to do so even as Christians. The messes in the closets of Christians are as gory as any. Child abuse, adultery, deception, greed, lust . . . and things I can't mention because this book isn't guaranteed unconditional acceptance. In therapy they can finally emerge, be faced, begin to heal because they are not moralistically condemned. The therapist doesn't say, "Bad girl! You broke the rules!" The therapist says, quietly, "This is who you are. This is what you've done. Tell me more. How do you feel? Am I shocked? No, I've heard worse!"

And unconditional acceptance can help the good boys and girls, whose sin is that they barely manage to move because they've determined never to do anything bad at all. It challenges them to risk, to step out, to believe that the first stumble, and the many after, can cause growth rather than consignment to hell. Truly the air turns sweet when such breezes blow.

Dependence, Differentiation

Moralistic conscience often intertwines with another dynamic: Separatists want authorities, parental and other, to be strong. We want to be able to count on their wisdom to guide us through life's snares. This easily becomes inappropriate dependence. "Tell me what to do! I don't know how to get through this myself. Help me!"

We're all tempted to remain children, to let grown-up people and institutions take care of us and fix our perplexities. By demanding unquestioning submission to its norms and expectations, separatism can easily slip into aiding and abetting rather than challenging this tendency. This is particularly pernicious when the human opinions of the authorities become equated with God's will. Any challenge quickly becomes a taunting fist raised against God.

When psychology meets the dependent, childish people such thinking can create, it offers a different message. The antidote is autonomy, individuation, differentiation, even maturity. The message is this: It's good to grow up. And the way you grow up is to assert your own style, your own personally grounded vision. You grow by questioning, challenging, sifting through the authoritarian injunctions to find what's helpful and reject what's not. You become a differentiated, "different-than" person not bound by every whim of the group—even though you recognize you're deeply shaped by and connected with the group.

Oppressive Expectations, Self-Actualization

One way authoritarian structures damage is by fostering heavy expectations. When a woman burns her life away giving herself endlessly to the poor clients she meets at her social work agency, and she does this because her background taught her to serve others unto death if necessary, she is a victim of oppressive expectations. Christianity, rooted in a core story of one who saves by dying and calls others to follow in his cross-aimed footsteps, turns easily oppressive. Virtually *any* expectation, no matter how sour or neurotic, can be justified by saying, "If Jesus (and all the other countless martyrs of the faith) could die, you at least can teach Bible school! Or clean up your room. Or be nice to your aunt no matter how much you hate her."

Psychology's antidote is to insist that people have a right to self-actualization. They have a right to nourish themselves, to experience their needs and try to meet them, to express themselves creatively. You have a right to be you, the counselor says. Though it's easily stereotyped as such, this isn't necessarily counsel toward selfishness. Abraham Maslow once defined it as "the full use and exploitation of talent, capacities, potentialities, etc."[6] Self-actualized people are fulfilled, functioning to the peak of their abilities. To actualize yourself is to transcend oppressive expectations so you can freely and fully give yourself to the world. You give yourself not because someone *expects* you to but because you *want* to. Not pinched self-denial but joyous self-expression is fostered.

Repressing Evil, Accepting the Shadow
Christians are supposed to be good. We're supposed to do good. We're supposed to want to be good. What do we do when we're bad? Sometimes we repent. But what do we do with all the known, half-known, and unknown urges, dreams, and stirrings that fall somewhere in that nether world between good and evil? What do we do with lust felt but not yielded to, bitterness welling despite all attempts to resist, violence that glares from eyes that smile, kind words that mask the unconscious hope of getting something from the other?

What we do with it, according to Carl Jung's psychology, is repress it. We pretend it doesn't exist. Actually we mostly don't even pretend, because we make the decision to repress at such a deep level we don't fully know we're making it. Unfortunately, though we may experience ourselves as striding starched and clean and free from sin through an upright life, we trail behind us a shadow. Step by step it slinks along, just behind, mocking us with drunken step and leering eye. John Sanford, one of Jung's Christian interpreters, defines the shadow as the dark, feared, unwanted side of our personality. In developing a conscious personality we seek to embody in ourselves a certain image of what we want to be like. Those qualities that could have become part of this personality but are not in accord with the person we want to be, are rejected and constitute the shadow personality.[7]

Psychologists argue the validity of the concept of shadow, a concept not easily subjected to empirical verification. I've found it, however, to be a helpful way of understanding the frequent coexistence of conscious Christianity with unconscious evil. It makes sense to think that rigid, separatist Christianity often strengthens the shadow by defining many feelings, thoughts, and behaviors as unwanted, inappropriate, sinful, condemned by God. Separatism typically offers no alternative but repression of negatives followed by expansion of the shadow.

Sanford notes two ways this causes harm: First, the potential for good buried in our shadow is lost. Second, we'll likely project our unacknowledged shadow onto others.[8] Suppose a man struggling daily with uncontrollable sexual fantasy watches vigilantly for signs that the minister has dirty thoughts—and pounces viciously on the first shred of evidence. Projection is what explains this odd, paradoxical behavior. Our friend sees in the minister what he can't face in himself.

What's the cure? Recognizing and accepting the shadow, says Jungian psychology. When the lustful thought, the angry urge, the vindictive fantasy arrives, we don't just kick it under the bed. We let it come; we don't become obsessed with squelching it.

We also look for better ways to use the energy driving the negative urges. The lustful thought flows from *eros*, a legitimate form of love which prompts us to relate to others. We can use that energy for appropriate relating, although we'll usually need to discard its initial form.

Anger often flows from a sense of violation. It can provide the energy to correct the violation or make peace with our perceived violator. Similarly, we can gradually nudge the vindictive fantasy toward reconciliation—even as we allow our spiteful scenario to play itself out.

When we use such approaches, the shadow gradually loses its power to corrupt. It instead enriches and energizes our lives. We no longer repress our negative energy and force it into hidden corners of our soul where we can't control it. We no longer use up half our remaining energy making sure neither we nor others catch a whiff of the heinous secrets buried under our pious demeanors. We can instead use *all* our energy, positive and negative, for good.

An important qualification is that we are *not* to *express* our shadow urges in their naked forms. There's a difference between being tempted and yielding, between unbidden lust, anger, or spite and their willful cultivation. I'm not urging that we abandon ourselves to the endless list of shadow drives. I'm simply saying we're not bad people when the "bad" urges come. We can therefore relax when they come. We can take the time to calmly and lovingly learn how to transform the urges into good things rather than shrieking and running for our lives at the first hint of their appearance.

The Limits of Psychology

Now it's crucial to note that the fresh breezes I've been so enthusiastically describing blow *through* the separatist house which keeps them in check. They don't replace it. While I tread here on speculative ground, it seems to me there was a time, as Western culture emerged from centuries of rigid, legalistic moralizing, when the entire culture benefited from such fresh breezes.

But gradually the breezes overcame the original structures. They weren't by themselves viable substitutes. I wonder if a startling change in the type of pathologies therapists have seen in the past generation or so is evidence of this. Donald Capps notes that "many psychoanalysts agree that the narcissistic personality is the predominant character type seen in therapy today, replacing the obsessive-compulsive type of an earlier era." A key cause of narcissism is the inability to leave behind the early childhood experience of being admired and petted. Clung to is a "grandiose self." It considers itself deserving of such attention and is enraged when it doesn't receive it. It makes its lifework manipulating others to get it and resists acknowledging limits.[9]

Could this in part be the result of unconditional acceptance, differentiation, self-actualization, and acceptance of the shadow run amok? Could it be that as such psychotherapeutic notions come to dominate—rather than leaven—a culture, they breed narcissism and cultural self-destruction? Could it be that such notions are healthy *only* when they enliven and soften rather than replace a house constructed of strong moral and religious values?

If so, cultural trends foreshadow what will happen to Christians if they dismantle their house in favor of psychology.

Unconditional acceptance will become sinning boldly that grace might abound. Let the chips of immorality fall where they may.

Differentiation will become an idolatrous radical autonomy which sees the unlimited self as god.

Self-actualization will become an idolatrous, God-rejecting search for one's highest self-expression regardless of its impact on others.

Acceptance of the shadow could become what it did unacceptably become in Jung's (not his Christian interpreters) psychology: an amorality which sees salvation as integrating into yourself all your facets, whether good or evil. Behaviors which contribute to this integration will then be proper, even if wrong by Christian standards.

This suggests the need to control the influence of psychological and other secular ideas on the biblical world in which we're trying to remain. How? We can accept those ideas which help us recapture truths buried in Scripture but which, as our Christianity has rigidified, we've lost. Other ideas, however, can't be squared with Scripture. We need either to abandon these or remind ourselves constantly that we're engaged in dangerous experiment which never allows relaxation.

Using Psychology to Recapture Biblical Truth

Let me turn now to four examples of (a) using psychology to recapture scriptural truth and (b) using Scripture to place limits on psychology. I will pair the four psychological insights described above with their possible scriptural analogues.

Unconditional Acceptance and Grace

In many separatist settings, including Mennonite ones which stress ethical living, the word of grace is uttered. Through God's grace, that unmerited forgiveness earned by Jesus dying for our sins on the cross, we're made new. We can put out on the curb the trash stashed in the closet of our life and piled high behind the door we've slammed on it.

But now we had better not put any more trash behind the door. We had better keep the closet clean. We must put only good, fine things in it—and keep them orderly. This understanding of grace offers much. It recognizes that grace, truly internalized, both prompts and empowers a response. The person offered grace *wants* to change and receives the *means* to change.

The problem with this version of grace is that it's paired with the high expectation that creates moralistic conscience. This destroys much of its power.

Unconditional acceptance is that empathic, nonjudgmental interaction with another which heals and frees. It opens eyes to see and reclaim this lost power.

Regular practice of unconditional acceptance helps us ask whether the Bible pairs expectation with grace as quickly as we do. The answer, I think, is that sometimes the Bible does. That's why it's so easy to fall into that approach. But sometimes the Bible gives grace a twist of radically freeing meaning that we easily miss until unconditional acceptance alerts us to its presence.

In Galatians 5:1, Paul has just concluded a complex discussion of the relation between law and our adoption through Christ as children of God. He then says, "For freedom Christ has set us free; stand fast, therefore, and do not submit again to a yoke of slavery." Later he adds that circumcision, a symbol of all rules, regulations, and driven moral behaviors through which we try to buy favor with God, isn't what counts. "Faith working through love" is what counts (v. 6).

Romans 14 offers a fascinating discussion of the Christian's freedom to do what's right for him or her. One person eats anything; another vegetables. One esteems one day as special; another all days. Though the need to respect the weaker one limits such freedom, it's nevertheless genuine and radical.

Many other Pauline admonitions seem to say we're freed, under the Spirit's guidance, to follow the law of love rather than a set of enslaving rules. Understanding Paul's concept of grace and freedom in Christ is no simple thing, but he does seem to endorse a version of Christian unconditional acceptance. He frees us to follow the urgings of our deepest, God-shaped beings. He frees us from the "goodness" of mere rule-keeping as if we were children trying to please a harsh parent by remembering every picky command.

Unconditional acceptance also helps us see the grace throbbing in Jesus' approach to people. Jesus criticizes those who think they need no grace because they've committed no sin. He's constantly in trouble for his too-easy acceptance of the sinners he so often befriends.

Perhaps nothing better exemplifies Jesus' stance than his telling of the story of the prodigal son.[10] Not a word in the text calls explicitly for the wayward son's repentance. There is simply the joyous recognition that the son has returned. It's precisely this too-easy acceptance of the lost son that enrages his elder brother.

It doesn't seem farfetched in such instances to see Jesus playing the role of the empathic, unconditionally accepting therapist. He plays a therapist who recognizes God has given us an inner drive toward wholeness. This drive emerges most fully and joyously when another's love frees us to find it for ourselves, through stumbles and falls. In contrast, when higher authorities *impose* wholeness on us, they create consciences terrified of failure. They immobilize us.

Unconditional acceptance helps us find grace even in the Old Testament, which we so often see as a collection of rules from that higher authority called God. An important aspect of unconditional acceptance is that no revelation, no matter what bad thing we reveal, is likely to cause the therapist to end the relationship.

We see that God stays in relationship with Abraham, Isaac, and Jacob. This is the triumvirate with whom God will eventually become indelibly associated. Yet each of these three giants of the faith (and virtually every other man and woman the Old Testament mentions) is deeply flawed. All lie and cheat and manipulate their way toward salvation. But God breaks relations with none. This again suggests God uses us, flaws and all, to move God's story forward. We needn't live brittle little lives whose only goal is to avoid the inevitable messes we flawed sinners make of our lives.

Now if I were to push the point further, and say that Paul, Jesus, and the Old Testament God simply offer unconditional acceptance, caring not a whit how we live, I'd be blaspheming them all. They clearly do care. Grace is a way of redeeming failure. It's a way of having a primary relationship with God our Lover rather than a primary relationship with rules. It's *not* a refusal to care about right living. Unconditional acceptance's tendency to slip into an amoral tolerance is what makes crucial grace's priority over it. It helps us find hidden meanings of grace. It's no fit replacement for grace.

Differentiation and Self-Criticism in the Bible

We often use the Bible to squelch differentiation, the growth of mature individuals who can question inherited beliefs and ways and stand on the strength of their own convictions. Valuing differentiation, however, helps us see that such squelching ignores instances in which the Bible records criticisms of traditional ways and movement beyond them. It also helps us recognize that modern critical perspectives aren't entirely alien to the Bible.

Abraham settled down to a safe, traditional life in Ur. Then he heard God telling him, at age seventy-five, to pull up stakes and set out for a new land.[11] Later, when God threatened to destroy Sodom, Abraham turned critic, arguing that God should save Sodom.[12] He didn't win, but God took Abraham's critical stance seriously.

Many centuries later the ways Abraham's new, critical attitude helped create had hardened. "I despise your feasts, and I take no delight in your solemn assemblies," Amos heard God saying.[13] Again there was movement caused by challenging and questioning the old ways.

The New Testament reveals a Jesus who constantly challenges. We're not made for the Sabbath, the Sabbath is made for us. Therefore we can sometimes challenge the sanctity of the Sabbath for the sake of a higher good, such as healing.[14] People who think themselves good may be the worst sinners. Sinners may most quickly enter the kingdom of heaven. A differentiation willing to see life in new and creative ways, even when it challenges everything held dear by the traditionalists, is woven into every molecule of Jesus' being.

In a similar way, Paul leaves behind the old ways that made him murder Christians. He combines the Spirit's guidance with his understanding of the story of Jesus to weave a strong new Christian theology.

All these examples, and countless more, urge not an infantilization of people, not the creation of cowlike herds who go wherever higher authorities prod, but the shaping of genuine adults. I, at least, couldn't see this until helped by psychological concepts of differentiation.

But the Bible clearly rejects differentiation in the form of radically autonomous individualism. The Bible's new ways try to recapture, in new forms, the essence of the old ways. They're not ungrounded and individualistic declarations of independence. They capture new ways of being in community, not new ways of standing alone.

Self-Actualization and God's Call

Self-actualization, frequently misunderstood as selfish self-expression, is often thought to be clearly *not* present in the Bible. But if we can see self-actualization as the highest development of a God-given self, then it may represent faithfulness rather than selfishness.

When I look at the Bible through self-actualization lenses, I see anew something I might otherwise miss:

the many stories of God calling individuals to do this or that with their lives. At the burning bush God tells Moses his calling. We could see this as God telling Moses that for him to actualize his self he must go to Pharaoh and lead the people out of slavery. Isaiah, Jeremiah, Ezekiel ... before them too God burns, calling them, telling them how to actualize their deepest selves. Jesus hears the call to be God's beloved Son, with whom God is well pleased. Then Jesus appears to Paul on the Damascus Road to tell him how to actualize his life.

I don't claim there's an exact match between call and self-actualization. I *do* believe they enrich each other. On the one hand, I experience myself as having an inner self which craves expression. Self-actualization frees me to like and express that self. It helps me aim my life toward what fills me with satisfaction, fulfillment, purpose. Rather than being driven by oppressive expectations, it encourages me to "follow my bliss,"[15] my deepest joy. On the other hand, the concept of call helps me understand that it can be God who works through the dynamics of self-actualization.

Separatist homes can encourage belief that the person is nothing at best and evil at worst, that all inner urges and desires are twisted. They are to be repressed, not expressed. The fatal mistake is to see people as having selves which need to be *purged*. Self-actualization helps us see that we have selves desperate for *redirection*. When Jesus calls us to give up our lives to find them, he's not telling us to live pinched, crabbed, mean little existences in which we pounce murderously on any evidence that we do, in fact, have lives. He calls us, instead, to reshape the old material into creative new forms.

Self-actualization does turn problematic and deserves rejection when it becomes an easy, shallow rationale for doing whatever makes us happy. This clearly contradicts the Bible's portrayal of God's call, which may involve us in much suffering on the way toward finding our true fulfillment.

The best psychological understandings affirm the paradox that true self-actualization in a broken world has to involve suffering. They include it as part of following bliss. They echo Jesus' paradoxical pairing of taking up our cross *and* finding rest under his easy burden and light yoke.[16] What deserve rejection are the pop psychologies that break the link between suffering and the true self-actualization exemplified by modern giants like Gandhi, Martin Luther King, Jr., Oscar Romero, Desmond Tutu, or Mother Teresa.

Accepting the Shadow and ?

The shadow isn't easy to square with the Bible. For that reason I offer a question mark rather than a specific biblical analogue for it. I'll try to face honestly places it can't be squared with the Bible as well as places it can.

Sanford gives examples of ways he thinks Jesus' point of view recognizes the shadow. Take the story of the fallen woman who comes to Jesus while he's dining with a Pharisee. Jesus praises the woman who, having sinned much, can be forgiven much. He contrasts her with the Pharisee who, having sinned little, merits little forgiveness.[17] Sanford points out the paradox implicit in the story.

> To live out our shadow side, as the woman did, is to commit many sins. Jesus makes it clear that . . . this woman had to change her way of life. On the other hand, to play it safe, as did the Pharisee, and remain unaware of the potentiality for sin in us and our need for forgiveness, is to become cut off from our capacity for compassion and love. If we only play it safe in life, we never come to know who we are. Life must be thoroughly lived if we are

to become whole people, and it is better to be forgiven than righteous.[18]

Sanford also discusses Jesus' command in Matthew 5:48 that we be perfect as God is perfect. We interpret perfection as absence of "blemish, stain, or spot," whereas Matthew's Greek word *teleios* means "brought to completion." Jesus wants "our lives and personalities . . . to be brought to completeness, to the end goal for which they are destined." This requires that we recognize and deal with *all* parts of ourselves, including the shadow.[19]

Sanford believes Paul was aware of the shadow. He wrestles with it in Romans 7:15-20, as he agonizes over doing not what he wants but what he hates. But Paul mostly advocates repressing the shadow. "Paul repeatedly urges his congregations to think and behave only out of what we can call their light side." Sanford flatly says that "Paul's ethic takes away man's freedom."[20]

I think Sanford overstates his case. Paul's thinking is more complex than that, as my related discussion of Paul and grace shows. But to the extent Sanford correctly identifies a tendency in Paul, I'm not inclined therefore to dismiss Paul and flatly violate Scripture.

What I do here—and it won't satisfy all—is remain in uneasy dialogue. I'm not ready to affirm the shadow against Paul. Neither am I ready to relinquish those truths of the shadow which I've seen with my own eyes and experienced in my own soul. I do believe there is within me a dark side whose hold over me only deepens when I try to repress it. I cling to the tension and hope for further understanding.

Particularly in this shadow discussion I walk a thin line between admiring and rejecting psychology. That makes this perhaps the right place to note that the balancing act between Bible and world I advocate is a difficult one. What I propose is art, not science.

I *have*, however, tried to offer guidelines. Though not everyone will agree with the way I use them, I hope at least the general movement they suggest is agreeable and clear:

First, to give the biblical world *priority*.

Second, to *journey fearlessly* toward the wisdom offered by the nonbiblical world which, though flawed, remains God's world.

Third, to *test* that worldly wisdom by trying to fit it back into the Bible and

- keep what fits.
- jettison what clearly doesn't fit.
- hold in tension (in hopes of further clarity) what neither quite fits nor seems worthy of instant trashing.

I've tried to model working through that cycle using psychology as an extended example. There are a myriad other disciplines offering countless other insights which could be taken through a similar cycle. This suggests we can, while making sure the Bible provides the walls and shape of our home, finally build a home as big as creation.

And that's how we build a separatist home which stands solidly on the rock of the modern age *and* distinguishes itself from that age. This home offers a shelter neither separatism nor translationism, by themselves, can ever provide.

QUESTIONS FOR DISCUSSION AND REFLECTION

1. Do Christians have a plausibility structure that's somehow truer than any other? Or must we make the same leap of faith required of anyone who commits to a particular truth?

2. Can we reason our way to faith? Or must we first

make a commitment by faith and then clarify and test it through reason?

3. What roles do reason and faith play in your faith journey?

4. Is there a gap between the Bible and the perspectives and ways of experiencing life the contemporary world shapes in us? If not, explain. If so, what are examples?

5. Do you suffer from moralistic conscience? Would unconditional acceptance help? Why?

6. Does your church encourage dependence or differentiation? Do you like this or would you prefer it to change?

7. Do you experience oppressive expectations? Would encouragement toward self-actualization help? Why or why not?

8. Do you think you have a shadow? If not, why not? If so, do you think you should repress it or accept it?

9. Has our culture lost its moral compass?

10. Can there be a balance between using psychological and other "worldly" insights and being grounded in the Bible?

CHAPTER 5

Joining Separatism and Translationism: The Centered Congregation

I hope I've offered glimpses of the new home whose outlines I see glimmering, faintly but tantalizingly, across the trackless wastes. I hope it's clear that two key building materials are separatism and translationism. I hope the importance of using *both* those materials, so the home will be solidly rooted in the modern age *and* offer protection from the age's harsh elements, is evident.

What may be less clear, and it's a fuzziness I now want to address, are the details of how these elements might bond. Proper bonding is crucial. Like the two parts of epoxy glue, which are useless until joined, separatism and translationism must be properly melded to form brick and mortar walls no wolf can blow down.

We can see the nature of the bond, I think, by focusing on congregational life. My discussion will unfold in two basic parts. First I want to look at typical ways congregations which depend on either separatism or translationism structure themselves. Then I want to sketch out the structure that could flow from joining the two, and some of its implications and practical applications.

MODELS OF CONGREGATIONAL STRUCTURE: THREE OPTIONS

I could use many names and images to capture three basic ways congregational life is often structured. *Rigid boundaries, few boundaries,* and *the centered model* are three I'll choose. I'll enrich and clarify their meanings through a variety of synonyms. My choice of labels owes much to Paul Hiebert. He has been stimulating my thinking ever since I met his views in a short, simple, but profound article examining categories we might use to define who is Christian. Hiebert talks of bounded, fuzzy, and centered "sets."[1] I'll describe each under its proper heading.

Separatism: Rigid Boundaries

A bounded set, says Hiebert, is a "category created by listing the essential characteristics that an object must have to be within the set." Hiebert suggests that when we see *Christian* and *church* as bounded sets, we distinguish clearly who is *in* the set, category, or group —and who is *out*.

You know apples don't belong in the category *oranges*. You can also know whether George and Jane belong in the category *Christian* or *church*.[2] You know that George, who gives intellectual assent to his church's doctrine, and agrees to live his life by its rules, is in. You know that Jane, who admits to doubts about certain doctrinal statements, and drinks forbidden wine, is out.

Focusing on the way families structure themselves, Charles V. Gerkin gives a similar description of the "closed" family. Such a family functions according to carefully prescribed norms and expectations enforced by authoritarian parents. As self-enclosed as possible, it keeps a close eye on interactions with the outside world.[3] Closed families lock their doors. You knock to get in. You wait for an answer.

Without meaning to be critical, I'd identify my own family of origin as exemplifying this style. First, we were Mennonite during an era when Mennonites still drew sharp distinctions between themselves and the world. Two factors then deepened the closure. One was that, as a missionary family, we were members of one culture trying to survive in an alien culture. Our style was to maintain our boundaries against that alien culture so the family could be a place of rest from its strangeness. There were also many of us: I had eight siblings. We were large enough to create a little miniculture, with its own unique rules and expectations. Such factors created two very discrete worlds: "we in here" and "they out there."

Robert Jewett adds a biblical twist. Jewett's fascinating thesis is that the apostle Paul fits neither of the two categories into which people often squeeze him. He's neither an intolerant moralist nor the offerer of a "universalistic religion of grace" against legalistic Jews.

As part of his discussion, Jewett suggests Paul holds together polar opposites reflected in the first and second of the Ten Commandments. The first commandment is to have no other gods before us but the one true God. This commandment, by itself, stirs a positive passion. The passion flows from the exclusive, monogamous commitment God and God's people make to each other. God's transcendent guidance of the people against the finite idols always ready to seduce them is affirmed.

The first commandment can also create fanaticism. Those trying to uphold God's transcendence sometimes equate God's ways and their understandings of God's ways. They fall into *hubris*. They yield to the overweening pride of thinking they can capture God's transcendent ways, that they can be like God.[4]

Paul, Jewett thinks, sees such tendencies in "the legalistic proponents of Judaism." In Romans 2:17-20, for example, Paul offers a sarcastic description of those who think they know it all. Paul means to prick this balloon of arrogance. The point is that although it's crucial to live according to God's ways, no one but God knows *precisely* what those ways are. Jewett says those who ignore this fact are captives of "faith without tolerance."[5]

Taken together, the above perspectives capture some common tendencies of separatist congregational structures. They can foster passionate commitment to the one and only true God and God's ways. They can also imprison members within rigid boundaries which elevate doctrines, customs, rules, and language to the level of absolutes. This easily turns them into idols.

We might image this structure as a boldly drawn circle. The ink defining the circle is whatever the congregation holds dear. If you meet the conditions represented by the ink, you're inside the circle. If you don't, you're out.

Translationism: Few Boundaries

Hiebert says fuzzy sets lack clear boundaries. "Rather, there are degrees of inclusion within them. Things may be a quarter, a half or two-thirds inside the set. For example, a mountain merges into the plains without a clear boundary, and red into orange."[6] In fuzzy-set thinking the boundaries between "Christian" and "Buddhist" or "inside the church" and "outside the church" are muddy.

You could, perhaps, be a quarter Buddhist, an eighth Shinto, a ninth Hindu, and the rest maybe secular humanist. This kind of fuzziness is common, for instance, in Japan. Fundamentalist George can be in if he wants (though he probably doesn't). So can Jane, whether she drinks wine or not. And even Emmett, who's working on a mixture of mysticism, New Age faith in harmonic convergences, deep ecology, and a smattering of Christianity.

Gerkin's "random" family offers a parallel. The random family lacks "organizational structure or consistent regulation of family interactions. Individuality and spontaneity are given full expression and encouraged." Irregularity, life lived according to whim, with little regard for others, is the norm.[7] You leave your doors open, bathroom included.

Jewett might characterize this style as rooted in the second commandment. This commandment rejects worship of graven images and "deals with the universal human tendency to desire a finite definition of and control over transcendent deity."[8] This commandment prompts passionate avoidance of idolatry, even in its subtlest forms. It challenges Mennonites, for example, to face the possibility that traditional ways and ethnic customs have often degenerated into idols competing with the one true God.

In isolation, however, commitment to this commandment produces its own idolatry. It creates a paradoxical, idolatrous worship of idol-shattering relativism. The idol becomes the unwillingness to draw any boundaries, to make any moral decisions, to consider anything clearly right or wrong.

Jewett believes Paul understands the dangers of such relativism and addresses them in Romans 1:32. There Paul describes those who know they are practicing what God forbids yet not only engage in them "but actually applaud others who practice them." Such people reduce all truths to the same level. Then subjective preference calls the shots.[9] Norms are abolished. Everything is up for grabs. Chaos reigns. Any hope of establishing an uplifting moral center is lost. This is "tolerance without faith."

Translationism risks imposing this open, unbounded structure on its congregations. Absence of boundaries can be accompanied by an easily welcoming, open spirit, but the welcome is ultimately shallow. It doesn't mean much to be welcomed into a setting where all are equally welcome.

We might image this structure as a collection of near-random dots which represent whatever each participant in the group holds dear. If the particular configuration of dots you happen to stumble on catches your fancy, you're free to add your dot to the mix. Whether you're in or out isn't important—there's barely an "in" or "out" to consider.

Separatism and Translationism Joined: The Centered Model

The first two approaches to congregational structure focus on the boundaries—either their imposing presence or their radical absence. A third alternative focuses instead on a center and to some extent lets the boundaries take care of themselves. This is Hiebert's centered set.

> It is created by defining a center, and the relationship of things to that center. Some things may be far from the center, but they are related to or moving *towards* the center; therefore they are part of the centered set. On the other hand, some objects may be near the center but are moving *away* from it, so they are not a part of the set. The set is made up of all things related to or moving towards the center.[10]

Hiebert is making two crucial points. One is that what primarily counts is whether you want to relate to the center that defines the set. If you do, you're in, even if still distant from that center. This might be true of the troubled agnostic who is far from Jesus—the center of the Christian/church set—but wants to move toward Jesus.

The other (related) point is the direction of your

movement. You might be a person who tries to say and do all the right pious Christian things. But if your real concerns have nothing to do with Jesus, you're moving away from Jesus. You're in danger of leaving the set of those committed to be in relationship with him even as you look like the most godly of the godly.

Similar to this is Gerkin's "open" family. This family combines commitment to basic family values with a consensus-based style of functioning. Individual input is welcome but autonomy isn't idolized. "The system is open, freely spontaneous, and yet regulated and consistent."[11] The doors in this family are ajar. You're neither automatically closed out nor free to assume absence of boundaries. You combine respect for individual privacy with a welcoming, communal spirit.

Jewett's portrayal of Paul goes in a similar direction. He suggests Paul combines the strengths of the first and second commandments to achieve "strenuous tolerance flowing from vital faith." Paul weaves together passionate commitment to God as center of faith with equally passionate refusal to tolerate worship of doctrines, rules, and customs as graven images. Paul offers a tolerance grounded in God's love which, through Christ, welcomes all into God's fellowship. Such tolerance doesn't dismiss God's concern for ethical response to God's love. Nor does it degenerate into American pluralism's "grudging but polite admission that others should have the right to express themselves even if they are wrong."[12]

A congregation fostering this approach would create an odd but invigorating structure. It would look separatist and translationist and be neither. It would be separatist in its commitment to God but translationist in its lessened concern with boundaries.

Like separatism, the centered approach would have boundaries. Unlike separatism, the boundaries wouldn't be bold lines of a circle you crossed to get in. One might image the boundaries as flexible, dotted lines. You'd fall within the boundaries when your life looked like an arrow pointing at the center (God revealed through Jesus and offering power through the Spirit). You'd be leaving the boundaries when the arrow of your life reversed course, away from God.

IMPLICATIONS OF THE CENTERED MODEL

So much for preliminary definitions. Now I want to discuss the centered model's implications for a variety of issues most congregations confront. I'll look at the bounded/separatist and unbounded/translationist approaches to each issue. Then I'll show how the centered model might, in each case, release the better qualities of both.

Conversion

Conversion makes a fitting first issue. The *bounded model* tends to view conversion as an either/or thing. Either you have or you haven't given your life to Jesus. What it means to do this may also be sharply defined. Such language as, "I accepted Jesus Christ as my personal Savior on August 3, 2004" (I don't want this book to get outdated too fast) may be required. If you can say and mean the words, you're Christian. If you can't, the congregation can be clear about the matter: You remain an infidel.

This can be a rigid, formulaic approach which cheapens the meaning of conversion and ignores the complexity of human responses to God. If you allow only this formula, and no other, then you have constructed a graven image. This contrasts with the Bible's use of many images and words to describe conversion.

The approach also holds power. It recognizes that we do face a choice between many gods, many idols. It properly forces us—even as it risks its own idolatry—to choose which god we will serve. It knows if we're not asked to make a choice we'll likely worship such gods as Money, Sex, Power, Security, Affection, Wealth, Loved Ones, Science. . . .

The *unbounded model* believes in conversion (if at all) through osmosis. If by chance you fall into a situation which has Christian overtones, and if something about those overtones appeals to you, some of it may rub off on you. This approach offers weak defense against the seduction of other gods and idols. It's critical of all passionate commitments except the commitment to make no passionate commitments. This can lead to a despairing, nihilistic, confused drifting.

But that same opposition to passionate commitment, though destructive when idolized, helps shatter arrogance. It challenges all fanatics who think their conversion formulas represent the only door to heaven.

The *centered model* insists on a choice for or against God through Jesus *and* humble recognition that no one owns the God whose ways are above our ways. It knows no one may dictate with absolute assurance how we do or don't get to God. It simply asks this of us: Do we, in whatever words or images most fully describe our commitment, agree to turn our life toward God and away from all false centers?

While the agnostic part of my Christian walk is lessening, it still exists. It was once dominant. I owe my being a Christian to the centered understanding of conversion. The bounded approach didn't work. The formulas never meant anything to me. I tried making my commitment through them, but nothing life-transforming happened. Then I tried the unbounded approach. I tried having no particular boundaries and no particular center. That left me cold, sad, lonely, unfulfilled. I gazed at a sky whose stars couldn't guide me because I didn't believe there was any home toward which they could point me.

Finally I tried making a simple commitment to point my life toward Jesus as a way of pointing through him to God. I would accept whatever meaning that offered me as I walked step by step. I wouldn't force myself to accept empty formulas or doctrines.

I've been taking those steps now for many years, and lo, my faith (I say this in all sincerity, pious overtones and all) has become to me more precious than gold. The separatist choice I made was crucial. So was the translationist refusal to be bound by formula. Thus is formed the bond, that strong epoxy of centered model conversion.

Church Membership

Closely connected with conversion is church membership. In the bounded model, church membership comes when one crosses the boundary into the inner circle. The membership applicant must accept whatever the boundary consists of before the circle will open to include him or her. People within the boundaries may turn tyrannical and self-righteous. They may claim the right to decide who of those standing outside may come in and who may not. Arrogantly equating their judgment with God's, they may sadly suggest that the person left outside the congregational home remains also outside God's home.

This approach does incorporate an important positive feature, however. Robert C. Worley helps identify it. He says all congregations have a "manifest culture." He defines this as "a set of perspectives on the different areas of congregational life, such as mission, maintenance of the congregation, and social life." People are shaped by and contribute to this set of perspectives.

Congregations also have an underlay of "latent culture" which is in some tension with the manifest culture. As new people and forces and experiences erupt in congregations, they may offer the latent culture an opportunity to challenge the dominant culture. This can create unhealthy conflict and instability if mismanaged.[13]

Worley suggests that congregations can maintain a creative rather than destructive tension between these various factions and layers by taking in new members in "discriminate" rather than "indiscriminate" ways. Congregations can clarify their goals and purpose for being, then interact with potential members to decide whether both parties' goals and intentions are compatible.[14]

Bounded churches, though they overdo it, know how to do this. They try to be clear about their own values and expect members to uphold them. Churches trying to take the Bible into the world will certainly need this skill.

In the unbounded model, mere desire to be a member suffices. Membership simply indicates desire to affiliate with this particular congregation made up of these particular people. It has little moral, biblical, doctrinal content. Members can drift their merry way to nowhere.

The good here is offering people a place to belong without exacting a heavy price for belonging. People can breathe whatever fresh doctrinal, theological, or other air they need to breathe to be healthy. In short, freedom is offered. And freedom, while idolized in North American culture, is nevertheless needed if people are to grow into seasoned adults and not remain submissive automatons.

The centered model works simultaneously at freedom and discrimination. The image of the Christian way as a *journey* is key to this. The bounded model properly insists that church membership requires commitment to values. But it promotes a static commitment to a collection of "either/or's." Although the unbounded model offers freedom, it promotes no particular movement. It's also static.

The centered model calls members to journey toward a specific destination (God) and face soul-toughening, value-deepening obstacles on the way. It also offers freeing movement and surprises. When you ask someone to accompany you on a journey toward Jesus, you do define a destination. You also acknowledge humbly that neither of you can know all that will happen on the way. This helps control idolatrous tendencies.

The centered model thus does insist on one central requirement for membership: following Jesus—or words to that effect. It wants clarification of congregational directions. It expects some compatibility between the congregation's and the applicant's commitments. But it doesn't make a rigid boundary of congregational goals. It offers them so congregation and applicant can, in mutual dialogue, decide if they're basically journeying toward the same center.

The way I've worked at this as pastor is to tell applicants their congregation expects them to see the journey toward God as their central commitment. Then I—and other congregational members—share specific ways this commitment has shaped the congregation. Congregational statements of faith or covenants of membership may summarize the congregation's understanding of what commitment to Jesus entails.

Finally, we don't want such statements ignored (unbounded model). We don't want them slavishly submitted to (bounded model). We simply want to know that they represent the general direction of the applicant's journey and will shape (and be shaped by) her or him.

Gentle Authority

This leads naturally to discussion of authority. The bounded style polices the boundaries and enforces the norms that keep members clear about what is in and out, right and wrong. The Bible, tradition, congregational-governing bodies, and pastors are the law enforcers. They offer rule books and lists of precedents. They hand down legal judgments, write tickets, and expel congregational criminals. Hierarchical imposition of authority is the norm.

This can produce a kind of Christian totalitarian society. But it also offers something all people need, particularly at earlier stages in their journey. It creates a clear, predictable structure people can count on to provide guidance and make and enforce decisions.

The unbounded model's authority is likely to be weak and fragmented. The very essence of the unbounded congregation is anti-authoritarian and anti-hierarchical. It verges on anarchy. Suspicion of any power, any authority, runs high. The individual wants to retain autonomy. The plus here is the ability to keep power in check, to recognize that Bible, tradition, church council, and pastor can all be oppressive clubs. Plenty of us pastors think we're God. Here's a pin to pop our arrogance.

The centered model both allows for the presence and exercise of authority and guards against its excesses. Authority is neither weak and irrelevant nor dedicated to guarding boundaries.

Let me illustrate from my own approach to preaching. I could preach to strengthen boundaries. Then I'd tell people clearly, sternly, unmistakably what constituted right and wrong behaviors, attitudes, feelings. I could preach to make people feel good—start with a few jokes, tell nice stories, move to an upbeat conclusion.

I do some of both. But mostly I try to articulate, as clearly as I can, the center of my personal and our communal faith. I share a faith grounded in the Bible, that road map pointing us toward Jesus. I hope this prompts people to move toward that center, but it's an invitation to freely chosen growth. It's neither an offer of aimless freedom nor a command to shape up or else.

This suggests congregational authorities need be neither judges nor jolly and irrelevant or amoral companions. "Guides" is perhaps most deeply what they are. They neither abdicate leadership nor arbitrarily infringe on their fellow-journeyers' freedom to travel as they feel led. They offer a gentle authority.

Communal Discernment

A subpoint of gentle authority deserves mention. There are many legitimate calls these days for a style of congregational decision-making and journeying that majors in communal discernment. The centered model virtually demands this style. If the preacher or other authorities aren't setting clear boundaries, yet direction is desired, the whole community, the whole congregation, will have to get involved. Leaders in this model can help focus issues and concerns. But then they must yield to a consensus-building group process in which people pull off at the gas station to check the map and see what route to take next.

Dealing with the Shadow

A second subpoint is this: the centered model offers creative resources for dealing with our shadow side (Chapter 4). In unbounded groups, shadow impulses easily run amok. The group allows destructive expression of impulses which should be acknowledged but not acted out. For example, sexual energy runs high in any group, Christians included. Hiding from this may simply drive its expression into the closet. But welcoming it easily degenerates into inappropriately expressing it. Spouse-swapping is simply not the way to go.

Bounded groups have a different, rarely recognized problem: Those who discipline deviators from the boundaries have their own shadows. They may choose discipline strategies prompted by their own problems. Let's suppose the pastor in a bounded congregation patrols the boundaries. He (most likely the gender in this case!) discovers that a member is abusing a daughter. It so happens that this pastor has abused his own children. Now when this sinful pastor discovers the same sin in the parishioner, he throws the book at him. He unmasks the sinner before the whole horrified congregation. The abuser is evicted. "Out, out with you, accursed one! Be gone!"

What has happened? The pastor, unable to face his own shadow, projects it on another. He scapegoats and casts him out to gain release from his own sin.

This is wrong. Yet it's a danger any bounded group faces, including Mennonites whose "believers church" commitment to a pure fellowship has historically inclined them to cast out offenders. The shadows of those who discipline may cause them to sin in the very act of judging the sin of another!

The centered model doesn't abolish but does lessen such tendencies. It permits a disciplining function, but the aim is more to encourage proper movement toward the center than to evict offenders. In some cases, perhaps, member and congregation must face their movement toward different centers. If they become arrows pointing in opposite directions, excommunication may be appropriate.

The centered model will, however, rarely make sin a boundary issue. It therefore makes scapegoating and eviction of sinners difficult. And because of its commitment to communal discernment, it places some checks and balances on the disciplining function. The pastor may have a key role in handling major deviations from movement toward the center, but the congregation will also stay involved. And if one sin particularly gets a pastor's goat, members not activated by this specific sin can question whether the pastor is viewing the sinner through clear and merciful eyes.

Strengthening the Center

I've said much about how we might relate to the center. Now I want to say more about the center itself. As I've indicated, the center toward which we journey is ultimately the Trinitarian God. That's the irreducible minimum. Putting God at the center and leaving the matter there is likely to satisfy no congregation, however. Its members will need to know practical implications of putting God at the center.

My purpose here isn't to give a detailed list of specifics. Rather, I want to suggest two kinds of things we might put into the center through preaching, congregational dialogue, and the statements of faith or covenants of membership I mentioned earlier: rules and stories.

Rules

Despite all my suspicion of rules, I believe they have their place. Congregations, through Spirit-led consultation with the Bible, the historic Christian tradition(s), and their own denomination, need to articulate rules or principles they consider important to the Christian life. To avoid such articulation is to capitulate to the secular individualistic ethos. When communities offer no communal guidelines, the task of ethical discernment falls entirely on individuals.

If our individual perspectives are truly shaped first by social, communal forces, this is a poor strategy. The community *must* create plausibility structures which support the moral values it considers central. This is how individual consciences receive the raw material they need to develop a moral center.

Such theories of moral and faith development, as are offered by James Fowler or Neill Q. Hamilton differ in details.[15] But they agree that we need different types of moral guidance at different stages in our life journey. Children sometimes need clear rules, whether they understand the "why" behind them or not. "Don't!" Period. All of us retain a child within who sometimes needs to rest simply on "Don't!" or "Do!" That's why congregations need to put some clear rules in their central affirmations.

Note, however, that the rules belong primarily in the center, not at the boundaries. The congregation says, "These are our central principles. We strongly encourage ourselves to grow toward them." This is a different strategy than, "These are the rules. Obey or leave." Freedom remains even as clear directives are offered.

This allows those who have grown to an adult stage of faith—in which they can be trusted to make decisions on the basis of internalized principles—to function at a level appropriate to their development. If they haven't reached such a stage, it encourages them to do so. In this way both infant and adult moral needs are simultaneously met. Milk and meat are together offered.

Stories

Stories, it should come as no surprise, also help strengthen the center. By telling stories that implicitly convey moral values, we help fill our imaginations and characters with moral fiber. We also keep the complexities and ambiguities that characterize real-life struggle with moral issues. It's one thing to say (as I believe) that Christian participation in war is wrong. It's another thing to tell a story of how someone's Christian growth forced this conclusion and what the implications of living it out were. In the world wars, Mennonites were sometimes jeered at, imprisoned, and tortured for their pacifist stance. Such real-life stories carry more weight than any pulpit indictment of war.

Stories particularly help put social morality into a congregation's center. Perhaps it says something bad about us North American Christians that we're so much better at making clear rules about personal morality than social morality, but that's the nature of things right now. And perhaps it's legitimate. Social issues are inherently complex. More harm than good would likely come of making clear rules about precisely how much income is immoral and whether microwaves and VCRs are tools of God or Satan.

And how would we make rules about how much complicity in environmental damage is too much? The mere act of letting an oil-leaking car go unfixed abets pollution, but the car's owner may be too poor to fix the leak the millionaire (with his or her immorally earned money) would never tolerate.

Yet creating moral passion about such issues is crucial. Stories can do that. I could tell the story of my own environmental concern, complete with its own complexities and ambiguities. How I've joined countless environmental organizations and regularly give money to them. How I've written environmentally concerned material for publication. How (more at my wife's urging than through my own initiative, certainly part of the story) we've created a backyard compost pile and recycle as much trash as possible.

I could also tell how I guiltily continue to drive my oil-burning and antifreeze-leaking '77 Dodge Colt, which I'm sure is doing no one any good. My '83 Subaru burns only gas (and very cleanly, my mechanic says, spewing only a quarter of the allowable carbon dioxide). But it leaks oil from a seal I can fix only by pulling the engine—which would use up money I'd rather send to environmental groups!

This story tells no one precisely what to do. It does, though, invite people to look at their own choices and wrestle in similar ways with moving—if only haltingly —toward a more environmentally sound lifestyle.

Homosexuality: A Case Study

At this point I want to offer an extended example of the way the centered model might affect the handling of homosexuality. I choose this issue because it's divisive and calls for more creative solutions than most congregations seem able to find. My approach isn't perfect. As a synthesis of opposing perspectives, it's open to criticism from both conservative and liberal or radical factions. But I think it might offer an alternative that transcends the typical complete rejection or complete acceptance stances.

Key to my approach is putting a congregation's stance on homosexuality in its center rather than at its boundaries. Now I don't want to get into a detailed discussion of what that stance might be. I want to focus on the most fruitful way a particular stance might be processed. Since I am writing for a Mennonite publishing house, and the Mennonite stance on homosexuality at this point is that homosexual practice is wrong, I'll assume that stance for this discussion. This needn't prevent finding a more creative approach than barring practicing homosexuals from our congregations.

Let's assume, therefore, that the typical congregation considers homosexual practice to be questionable. A typical result would be to make this a boundary issue. If you're a practicing homosexual, the matter is clear: You're out. Let's remember here Jewett's discussion of the second commandment's prohibition of graven images. Isn't it possible that making homosexual practice *the* deciding factor in whether you're in or out of the church (and, by implication, God's grace) turns it into a graven image?

I think so. That's why I advocate the centered approach. It would give a congregation full freedom to state belief that homosexual practice was wrong, if the congregation so concluded. But it would *not* make practice the deciding factor. It would say to the homosexual, "This is our stance. We're willing, however, to process this issue with you as one of us, as one who stands within the circle of this family of God. You needn't remain outside, in the cold, until this issue is resolved."

This stance wouldn't satisfy the homosexual who insisted on unconditional acceptance and affirmation of practice. Such a person might conclude he or she wasn't in any way moving toward this congregation's central values—and didn't want to be a member there.

But the homosexual willing to tolerate some challenge, willing to wrestle in some way with the potential brokenness of his or her situation, would be welcome. Not unconditionally welcome, but welcome. I realize this could leave everyone partly dissatisfied, needing to continue struggling and talking. But I think the imperfection would be worth the central benefit: granting homosexuals status as citizens of God's realm even as the discussion went on.

The congregation would benefit as well. Its members would, under such an agreement, be forced to deal with the pain and exclusion homosexuals feel. This could soften attitudes and create a congregation filled with the grace and mercy each of us (sinners all, fallen short of the glory of God) had better be willing to offer each other. Otherwise we too might find ourselves shortly outcast.

There are other many other issues I'd propose to handle in a similar way. Drugs. Divorce. Alcohol. Paying war taxes. Buying stocks of companies implicated in apartheid or armament production. Suppose a congregation deems each wrong. It can state this clearly, forcefully, passionately. It can also—by putting its passion in the center rather than on the boundaries—offer room for dissension, personal choice, freedom, and the growth thus bred. The congregation puts at its center commitment to take the world into the Bible. It also allows the world's fresh air to blow through its permeable, flexible boundaries.

Limits of the Centered Model

I believe, obviously, in the merits of the centered model. But it's imperfect. Let me mention some ways.

First, it's complex. It's fairly easy to image a congregation as bounded by a circle, being a collection of random dots, or being a relatively free community of arrows moving toward a strong center. It's easy to advocate the latter as the best. It's harder to consistently understand and live out the daily implications of continually holding together polarities usually allowed to go their separate ways.

Second, there are times for me, at least, when the centered model simply breaks down under the stress of real-life issues. The synthesis of separatism and translationism falls apart. Take willful participation in war. I'd just about put that on the boundaries.

Or take adultery. Having seen some of its destructive effects, I'm tempted to add it to the boundaries as well. This wouldn't mean a quick authoritarian decision when such practice is discovered. I've also watched people, given enough freedom, make their own free, adult decision to leave behind a destructive practice. How much more growth this promotes than would a command that cut off moral wrestling and said, "Daddy says you have to quit!"

But I do think that if, after plenty of nonjudgmental latitude is granted, no repudiation of such practice were discerned, the time might come for a congregation to lapse into the bounded model and say, "Here we stand. We'd like you to leave either this lifestyle or us." This is, of course (as I need to recognize), precisely what some people feel they must do with homosexual practice.

Third, I can't guarantee the centered model will

work in all settings. I've experimented with it enough to appreciate it deeply, but it needs more testing.

QUESTIONS FOR DISCUSSION AND REFLECTION

1. Have you experienced instances of the bounded approach to congregational life? Explain.
2. Have you experienced instances of the unbounded approach? Explain.
3. What is your response to the centered approach?
4. What kind of family did you come from or do you live in now? Do you see any way in which this helps you understand the way your congregation functions?
5. What rules do you think should be in the center of your congregational life?
6. What stories might you share that embody a struggle with or exemplify moral values?
7. What role do you think the "shadow" plays in church discipline? Can those who discipline be blinded by their own sin?
8. Do you have a bounded, unbounded, or centered approach to homosexuality?
9. How do you respond to the argument that the centered approach to homosexuality, which allows traditional *theology* to coexist with a freer congregational *polity*, offers a workable compromise?
10. Will the centered approach create a congregation whose moral stances are too weak, too strong, too complex, or just about right?

CHAPTER 6

One Way and Many Ways

After many chapters in which I've concentrated on how one might build a Christian home in a homeless world, I want to face pluralism head on. I want to ask how a particular Christian home relates to the many other possible homes. I'll ask that at two levels. The *intrafaith* level refers to the significant pluralism that exists *within* Christianity, the many different ways of being Christian. The *interfaith* level refers to Christianity's relationship with other ways, other faiths, other religious homes.

INTRAFAITH INTERACTION: THREE OPTIONS

Anabaptism, Protestantism, Roman Catholicism. A myriad denominations. Countless splinter groups. As many individual idiosyncrasies within those larger groups as there are stars in the Milky Way. How do we make sense of such plurality? I propose to do so simply by extending to intrafaith interaction the previous chapter's discussion of the bounded, unbounded, and centered models.

The Bounded Model
Those of us who function within the bounded model gaze out at the array of ways Christianity is understood and lived and come to a simple conclusion. The one

fully right Christian way is, of course, ours. When I was growing up I didn't know there could be any non-Mennonite right way.

The Unbounded Model

The divisions afflicting and weakening Christianity pain those of us attracted to an unbounded approach. Our style is to work at abolishing or at least fuzzing the boundaries which enclose groups and divide us from each other. We who champion ecumenical progress and consider denominationalism a sin, an evil fracturing of the body of Christ, belong at least partially here. We want to see Christians soften the passion—the sometimes angry and ugly passion—with which we defend and advocate the distinctives we hold dear.

We Mennonites who remove *Mennonite* from our congregational names or downplay our peace church stance to avoid offense are, at least in those particular areas, using an unbounded approach. This book contains evidence of such tendencies, as I try not to overstress those Mennonite peculiarities which might severely limit my audience.

The Centered/Contextual Model: One Center, Many Expressions

Now suppose we want to keep the bounded model's passion *and* the unbounded model's softer, more ecumenical tone. We'll want to turn, I think, to the centered model. It knows that all of us need a set of strong central statements, values, and affirmations to which we can commit ourselves. It also sees the human tendency to make idols of such affirmations. It therefore simultaneously promotes passionate affirmation *and* humble acknowledgment of finitude.

It says, for example (to paraphrase four distinctives J. Denny Weaver suggests contemporary Mennonites might affirm), "This is who we as Mennonites are. We're for *peace*, against war. We're for commitment to follow Jesus as *disciples*. This prompts us to live lives *separate* from the world, in the context of *community*.[1] It also says, "But we recognize that as others have sought to understand God's leading, they've made different affirmations. We respect and open ourselves to learn from those affirmations even as we remain committed to our own."

Now implicit in the centered approach is a crucial concept: *context*. Context also emerged in my discussion of the Bible and the need to connect biblical and contemporary contexts (Chapter 2). Plausibility structures (Chapters 3 and 4) come close to being a fancy way of talking about context. Here I want to focus on how we can simultaneously make unifying affirmations *and* take the varied contexts of the modern world into account.

Let me explain. The centered model stresses central *principles* it assumes all Christians will in some way affirm (such as the centrality of the triune God). It permits, however, a variety of applications or *expressions*. To put it another way, all people have roughly the same body shape. But how they dress and decorate those bodies varies wildly.

The centered model recognizes some irreducible body of Christian beliefs and practices all can affirm. But the clothes put on it will make it look very different in varying settings or contexts. *Context* then refers to those dynamics and forces that determine what clothes Christians will want to put on the body, what shape local application of general principles may take.

This understanding of context is coming especially from feminist, black, and third-world theologians who challenge traditional Western Enlightenment ways of doing theology. Westerners, they think, overestimate the possibility of developing an objective theology which transcends local contexts. The challengers want us to see that the Word never becomes flesh simply in a timeless, acultural way. It's always incarnated in particular events and situations and dynamics.

René Padilla makes the striking statement that "a photocopy of a theological document written in Europe and North America can never satisfy the theological needs of the church in the third world." He adds that it's time for a "theology that . . . shows the many-sided wisdom of God."[2] It's time to free the gospel from dependence on one context (Western) which has imagined itself to transcend all contexts. It's time, in other words, to adopt a centered model in which Christians affirm the one God even as they express this in a plurality of context-shaped ways.

A few years ago I wrote an article for a Mennonite denominational magazine. In it I suggested that the Jesus accused of being too cozy with gluttons, adulterers, tax collectors, and many other species of sinners would maybe today frequent country music bars and dance with the sinners there. He might even, I speculated, smoke an occasional cigarette with smokers, not because he believed in this but because fellowship with smokers might be more important to him than absolute purity.[3]

Now I could well have been wrong about all this. My concern isn't to reiterate questionable speculation but to ponder the meaning of the reaction which quickly flowed in to the magazine's letters section. On the one hand there were expressions of horror, shock, condemnation. I was asked to apologize to Jesus. The editor was chastised for allowing such garbage to appear in print. On the other hand, there was warmth, approval, empathy. Yes, said some, this was the Jesus they knew, the Jesus who cared for people no matter what their condition, no respecter of rigid moral boundaries when they prevented healing.

Why the dramatically different reactions? Did some respondents come from Venus and some Pluto? Were my opponents Christians and my supporters and I representatives of the antichrist? Or (as I'd prefer) vice versa? Was this simply a clash of different theologies? The latter comes closest, I think, but still begs the question of *why* such different theologies exist. The answer, I'd speculate, lies in differing contexts. This is no scientific analysis (and perhaps simply reveals my stereotypes), but my impression was that many critics came from small towns or rural areas, while many supporters came from urban areas like my own.

This suggests two specific contexts—urban and non-urban—which may shape our expression of Christianity. Let me examine a few others.

The Oppressed Context

In mentioning feminist, black, and third-world theology I've already implied one crucial context. Each of those theological streams flows from the one broad context of those who are in some way oppressed. Thinkers shaped by this context have offered many insights. Three strike me as particularly provocative (and amplify comments I made in Chapter 3 about the "community of outcasts").

Feminist Letty Russell stresses that we're "standpoint dependent."[4] How we see and understand Christianity depends on the perspective from which we approach it. Liberation theologians tell us that Bible and faith look very different from the underside of history than from the top. Speaking on behalf of poor and oppressed people in Latin-American and other third world countries, they claim to see that God has a "preferential option for poor people."

What this means is that God wants justice for all. To achieve this, God has to build up the justice supplies of poor people while drawing down the justice supplies of the rich. This doesn't mean God is against rich people, but rich people may think so because they have to give up so poor people can get.

When we look at the Bible from this standpoint,

what jump out are the myriad passages we rich people overlook or spiritualize. In countless texts the God revealed by God's dealing with the Israelites, by the prophets, and by Jesus clearly does love poor people and offers them special hope of redemption.

Another insight is the cruciality of *praxis*. This is a fancy way of saying "practice." Oppressed people don't have time to sit around in ivory towers and spin theories. When you're a poor peasant oppressed by rich growers of Dole bananas, you want pertinent applications of Christianity. Your Christianity will then grow out of reflecting on the meaning of your daily life, your daily praxis, or practice.

This emphasis on praxis helps focus attention on the political, economic, and social structures that shape daily living in oppressive ways. I once visited a North American Mennonite Sunday school class whose members were trying to take seriously the insights of Central American immigrants. I listened, dumbfounded, as immigrants with little formal education talked, nevertheless, of political forces and cultural clashes and the way the gospel addressed them. The context which shaped these people gave them unique insight into aspects of Christianity and culture their North American peers had never considered.

Feminists, particularly, stress a third insight. It involves the cruciality of respecting *personal experience*. For Russell this doesn't mean focusing merely on individual experience but on the total social context out of which individual lives emerge.[5] It means you need to know something about me and the social forces that shaped me (and vice versa) if we're to communicate in any significant way.

Recognizing the power of personal experience means unmasking the illusion that when Karl Barth, Paul Tillich, or Menno Simons write books and make theological statements they're communicating objective truth.

They aren't! I know little about the personal experience of Barth, Tillich, or Simons. I do know, however, that all reveal clues to the times, the settings, the personal events that shaped their theology.

I doubt, for example, that former priest Menno Simons and the Mennonites who were given his name would have tried (as they did) to reject all hints of Roman Catholic "corruption" had they not originally been Catholic themselves. Family quarrels are always the sharpest. Yet they—and we, with our modern foibles—would prefer to think we're stating unvarnished truth and not context-tinged truth when we take our stands. The point isn't that we never tell the truth. It's that the truth we tell is always colored by factors unique to our context. We'd better be humble, therefore, about just how universally applicable our particular understanding of truth is.

The Power and Affluence Context

As important as are the insights the oppressed context can offer us, many of us belong most fully to another context, the context of those with power and affluence. We need to understand and wrestle with a gospel that talks to us in different ways than to the oppressed.

I don't have solutions for our dilemma as wealthy and powerful people trying to live the gospel of a wandering rabbi with no stone for his head, who said poor people were blessed. I simply want to note this: We who own supermarkets, run banks, import Dole products, and write books on computers will experience our faith one way. Others of us offer food stamps at the checkout counter. We suffer bank foreclosures. We break our backs to harvest bananas and sweat over computer innards on a Korean assembly line. We'll experience our faith another way.

Enlarging Contexts Through Cross-Fertilization

To stress context's power to shape expression of faith is to risk affirming fragmentation. Each context, each separate little version of Christianity, does its own little thing. To some extent this is inevitable. The shaping power of context is an unavoidable given.

But I don't mean to leave things there. The centered model offers a more creative possibility. We can recognize that central Christian principles will indeed be expressed in varying ways. We can also learn new ways of being faithful in our contexts by noting how others have been faithful in *theirs*. Contexts can cross-fertilize each other, so each context can move toward an ever-fuller, ever-richer expression of the principles all share.

I've experienced such cross-fertilization myself. I can never fully escape my context as a white, male, affluent American. But I can learn much about being a better Christian in my context from those who are nonwhite, female, poor, members of other cultures. For example, as I sit at my Korean computer writing, I could use the power this gives me in several ways. I could simply reinforce my context. Or I could let the insights of oppressed people broaden my understandings. They could then help me share ways I (and those like me) could function more faithfully in my own context. This might include valuing the feminist emphasis on personal experience even though I'm male. Or recognizing the importance of letting my theology be shaped by daily praxis.

To summarize, then, I'm suggesting that we Christians possess a center that unites us. We express that center in the different ways our contexts dictate. We can transcend the walls of the particular room we occupy in the house called Christianity by visiting the tenants of other rooms. Together we'll build an ever-enlarging Christian home.

INTERFAITH INTERACTION: THREE OPTIONS

No matter how complex may be this business of letting different contexts shape different expressions of the one Christian way, they remain variegated expressions of one way. Now it's time to *really* complicate things. It's time to ask how the Christian way, the Christian center and the home it creates, might relate to other ways, other centers, other homes.

I begin with a true story.

"Dad," she wanted to know, "are we Christians or Jews?" She wanted to know this, my first-grader Kristy did, because she'd found out her classmate Karla was Jewish. She was Jewish and celebrated Hanukkah, not Christmas. And in her home there was a menorah, not a cross. I told Kristy we were Christian but felt odd trying to explain why to a little girl who knew only that the other little girl was her friend. Kristy would have been appalled to know how quickly adults stop liking each other when the labels slash their friendship.

A year passed, and the questions aged with it. "Dad," said Kristy, "does Karla's family believe in God?"

"Yes."

"Then why is there any difference between us?"

Oh, Kristy, this gets pretty complicated, trying to explain this to a second-grader in such a way that you can understand—yet without perpetuating the horrors religious imperialism has unleashed on the world.

Finally I said, "Well, Kris, the way I understand it is that a long time ago Jesus (who by the way, was a Jew) came—"

"Jesus was a Jew?! But I thought Jesus was a Christian!"

I sighed. Why couldn't they have worked this mess out two thousand years ago so I wouldn't be stuck explaining it?

"Well, yes, Jesus was a Jew, which I know is confusing, but let me try to explain. It seems this Jesus came, and he was kind of like a Jewish preacher. He told people what God was like and how to be friends with God. And he said that if you watched what he was like and the way he behaved, you'd get a picture of what God's like.

"But there was this problem, see. Some Jews thought they already knew how to be friends with God and didn't really need Jesus. Some other Jews thought you had to agree with Jesus' way for God to be your friend."

"Okay, go on," Kristy said.

"Now the Jews who weren't too happy about Jesus, and the Jews who were, got to arguing with each other. They argued so much they stopped being friends. The Jews who didn't want Jesus stayed Jews, and the ones who did want Jesus called themselves Christians. They started telling people who weren't Jews or Christians about Jesus and they became Christians, too. That's where our being Christian came from.

"But I have to tell you about an awful thing that happened just before I was born and while Grandma and Grandpa were already alive. Maybe partly because they were still mad about the fights Jews and Christians had so long ago, some Christians thought they were better than Jews. They thought Jews were bad people. They started doing terrible things to the Jews. They killed millions of them."

Kristy gasped. "They did? But that was a terrible thing to do! People should never do things like that to each other."

"It *was* terrible," I agreed. "The way I see it, we have to agree to think differently but still be friends with each other. It's never right to hurt and kill people no matter how much you disagree with them."

"Well, that's certainly what I think, too, and I'd never want to hurt Karla."

I share that anecdote at such length because it raises, at a basic level, the key issue I want to discuss at this point: how the Christian way should relate to the many other ways. Various theorists propose various ways one can summarize the options for addressing interfaith pluralism. I'll share some representative examples, boiled down, predictably enough, into the bounded, unbounded, and centered models.

The Bounded Model

Alan Race suggests the "predominant attitude of the church through Christian history has been to regard the outsider as in error or darkness, beyond the realms of truth and light." He calls this "exclusivism."[6]

Ted Peters' term is "confessional exclusivism," which takes this stance toward other religions:

> Once one confesses one's faith in the centrality of Jesus Christ and the absoluteness of the divinely inspired revelation in him, the religious insights of non-Christian traditions cannot be seriously considered.[7]

Harvey Cox talks of "antidialogic particularists." They "insist that all others must accept Jesus or be damned," citing John 14:6: "I am the way, the truth and the life."[8]

The bounded model is what I'll call this stance, whose approach to religion is predictable: Other religions lie outside the boundary of the one true way. There are nuances within this approach which can lead some to stand firmly for Christianity as the one true way without being nasty about it.

But this model wants nothing to do with any weakening of Jesus' claim to offer *the* way. I could have told Kristy our way was right and Karla's wrong. I could have said Karla and her family couldn't hope to relate to God without Jesus, and any relationship they thought they had with God was a delusion. That would have been a bounded approach.

The weakness here is that tendency toward arrogance and imperialism which *did* help slaughter six million Jews (though I know the causes of the Holocaust were complex). The strength, as Cox notes, is the reminder "that without the radical particularity of the original revelation, we would have no faith to share."[9]

The Unbounded Model

Race describes "inclusivism" as a stance toward other religions which regards them as possessing truth and being a "locus of divine presence." Although this stance fuzzes the boundaries between Christian and non-Christian truth, which moves it in an unbounded direction, it retains Christianity's primacy. The truths of other religions, it affirms, belong finally to Christ. This stance thus falls in a gray area between the bounded and unbounded models.

Karl Rahner, perhaps its most noted exponent, is responsible for the term "anonymous Christian." By that he means that whenever someone is seeking to relate to God, she or he unknowingly participates in the grace offered by the Christian God.[10]

What Peters calls "supra-confessionalism" clouds the boundaries further. Adherents of this stance believe there is one final divine reality which each of the world's religions partly grasps. Christianity is one of many manifestations of a religion higher than any of our current religions. This is the old "different roads up the same mountain" theory of religion.[11]

Cox describes the "many mansions" stance. It names those who think the many rooms in Jesus' Father's house (John 14:2) "refer to the heavenly places in which Hindus and Buddhists will dwell—alongside Christians—in the hereafter."[12]

Hans Küng talks of two positions which mirror each

other. Depending on your preference, either "all religions are equally untrue" or "all religions are equally true." Either stance abolishes all boundaries. It simply doesn't matter what you believe. Any belief is as bad or good as another.[13]

I label these approaches "unbounded" because all have fuzzy or nonexistent boundaries. I could have told Kristy that Karla was Christian only she didn't know it. Or that Judaism and Christianity are simply different ways of loving God. Or that it didn't really matter what you believe. Then my explanation would have fallen in this group. To a certain degree, since I was struggling with the right balance between exclusion and inclusion, Kristy might have heard my explanation in such terms.

The weakness here is the tendency to dissipate passion, conviction, to lose Christ, the firm center. The strength is the offering of a "universal dream." We need that dream, says Cox. Otherwise we "falsify the message and diminish the scope of the original vision."[14]

The Centered Model

I hope Kristy didn't hear my comments as unbounded, because I was trying to articulate a centered understanding of my faith. I meant to hold firm to the rightness and centrality of our family's commitment to Christ. I also wanted to remain open to Karla's truth and accept some Christian responsibility for the deadly Jewish/Christian squabbles.

Several sources articulate a stance compatible with the one toward which I'm heading. Cox's point in juxtaposing Jesus' way, truth, life, and many mansions statement was that we need to hold them together.

Peters likes

> confessional universalism. This position affirms the claims of the Christian faith but is open to the insights of other

faiths. It is confessional, because it affirms the gospel of Jesus Christ as borne through history by the Christian tradition. It is universal . . . because it regards its claims as ultimate (valid for all people of all times and places), . . . and because it believes that there is more truth to be learned and that dialogue has the potential for expanding our understanding.[15]

Lesslie Newbigin supports Peters. Newbigin argues that "the Christian goes to meet his neighbor of another religion on the basis of his commitment to Jesus Christ. There is no dichotomy between 'confession' and 'truth-seeking.'"[16] Newbigin gets me where I want to go. He's saying that we each have to choose a particular standpoint, a plausibility structure, a context, a basic center (to echo all the interrelated terms scattered throughout this book). From or through that center we then look for and test truth. Yet as that center sifts and tests new truth possibilities, it can keep growing and expanding with each new insight.

That's what makes this stance so productive. It combines the confessional passion of the bounded approach with the openness to new truths of the unbounded approach. It avoids both harshness and mushiness. It unflinchingly upholds a particular center but recognizes that we can incorporate into it truth organized around other centers.

This has some affinities with the various unbounded stances but differs in one way. The more radical unbounded approaches say that each religion is a home on a huge estate which is a super-religion. Therefore it doesn't matter if you mix the homes up. They're all part of the same reality.

The centered approach recognizes that even if this were true (and who can prove it isn't?) we have no way of dwelling in that larger estate except through our particular home. If we do try to dwell in the larger estate, the result, paradoxically, is to create our own little religion. What we do when we try to affirm a religion larger than a particular one is free ourselves to choose the truths we like. We create personal religions called Sheilaism or Michaelism or John Doeism. The idols of individualism and radical autonomy beckon. When we commit to one home, such as the Christian one, the wisdom of a tradition shared by millions and tested over millennia guides our understandings and choices.

Here I'm remembering Lindbeck's distinction (Chapter 3) between the experiential-expressive and cognitive-linguistic stances. The experiential-expressive understanding believes that religions are different ways of articulating the same depth experience, of entering the one grand estate. It would thus more easily accommodate unbounded approaches.

My approach is more cognitive-linguistic. Different religions, with their different grammars of faith or houses of being, shape us into different people with different understandings of life. We can't be shaped simultaneously in ten different homes without opening ourselves to chaos and fragmentation. We avoid fragmentation by bringing truths from other homes into our own, rather than trying to live in all of them at once.

This is how I make sense of Gandhi's contributions to my faith. Gandhi used the power of nonviolent love to overthrow the British while operating from a non-Christian center. He also, interestingly enough, used his own version of a centered approach as he let Christianity enrich *his* center. Yet his non-Christian life helps me see what a Christian's life could look like. Gandhi helps me visualize more clearly my own center —even though he wasn't moving toward my particular center and refused the Christian label.

Cox offers another example of taking truth from another house and fitting it into the Christian house. Tibetan Buddhists, he says, approach their deepest beliefs in a playful way they call "crazy wisdom." This can help us remember and appropriate the Christian Pauline idea of being fools for Christ.[17] Or it might remind us of the playful hyperbole that marked many of Jesus' parables and sayings.

We don't then become Tibetan Buddhists or see them as anonymous Christians. We instead let "crazy wisdom" make us better Christians. We recognize that each of our traditions is different, even as we let the truth of the one tradition evoke the truth of the other.

The aim, then, is to allow other religions to evoke more and more truths within our own. We add to our own house the truths other religions help us see. We don't tear down one of our walls here, borrow one of their walls there, and cobble together a syncretistic house that tries to be all religions and ends up being none. As we work at this, our house should, little by little, get bigger and bigger. It should one day be as big as the universe as it incorporates all truth into itself.

Now so far what I've been doing is looking at other religions from *within* Christianity. I've been saying that as we observe the world from the vantage point of our particular Christian commitments, this is how we might both maintain such commitment and remain open to other truths.

There's another vantage point I can take. I can look at Christianity from *without*, as a sort of neutral observer seeing Christianity merely as one of many religions.[18] When I do that, I'm forced to recognize there are many religions organized around many centers. What makes mine better than another? From outside, I can't answer. From outside, I can't even be sure mine *is* better.

Purely at the level of making a list of religions, then trying to choose from them, I wouldn't want to claim

Christianity's superiority. I'd want to grant to the Hindu, the Buddhist, the Muslim, that none of us can claim *a priori*, in advance, the superiority of our way. If we're to coexist without cramming each other's right way down the other's throat, sometimes killing the more recalcitrant resisters of our proselytizing, we at least have to grant each other that.

This may sound like I have, finally, yielded to pluralism and relativism. In a certain sense I have. As I indicated in Chapter 4, none of us can claim to capture absolute truth. We can only decide, by what is ultimately a leap of faith, which truth we'll allow to guide us.

But I resist relativism in believing that we do, based upon the better judgment and intuition of our total beings, have to make the leap. And once we do, then we live by the truth our house offers us. Then our way does become for us the better way—even as we remember that others see other ways as better.

We're forced to live within a paradox. On the one hand, our house says Jesus *is* the way, the truth, and the life. Although Jesus may have prepared many mansions for many others, our call is to live for Jesus.

On the other hand, even as we live for Jesus, we remember we could have made a different leap. We would then be in a different house, seeing things a different way. This forces us to respect the leaps others have made even though our choices differ.

I need to address two implications of this stance at this point. One is the possibility of building an overarching structure that binds people of the world together despite their diversity. The other is evangelism.

Building an Overarching Structure

What I've been saying could be read as simply entrenching pluralism more deeply into the fabric of the modern world. If our task isn't to force all people at all costs into a Christian home, how do we find any common ground for coexisting with each other? Harvey Cox and William H. Willimon suggest ways we can affirm both particularity and a unifying universalism.

Cox says all world religions have both a particularistic and a universalistic pole. "Each nourishes . . . its own unique and highly particular vision. . . . The particular hub defines the center around which each world faith rotates." Each also "generates a universal vision." The Koran calls for a unified human family. "The bodhisattva compassionately refuses to enter nirvana until every sentient being can enter with him." Christ reveals a God who yearns for "an inclusive community of service and praise."[19]

Willimon argues that, as a Christian, his task isn't to seek some generalized human unity that will overcome the divisions threatening nuclear holocaust. His call is to affirm the truth he finds in Jesus—because it's precisely this truth that makes him care about those whom nuclear war would destroy.[20]

We don't need to divest the world of its particularities. We need passionate commitment to a particular vision which then drives us back out in love for all the world.

This has implications beyond the interfaith realm. It suggests the antidote to all the individualistic and pluralistic fragmentation that afflicts us isn't merely to impose one vision on all. More workable might be an approach in which individuals and groups looked for the universalistic, unifying tendencies hiding within their own traditions and allowed these tendencies to drive them back out into concern for all. We might, for example, unite to promote world peace, end hunger, and save our global environment—while grounding such common vision in our many unique traditions.

Evangelism

To address evangelism, let me go back to the different models.

The bounded model simply tries to convince people committed to other ways to change their way for Jesus' way. Some groups do this gently and lovingly. Others are willing to use any number of coercive tactics, even brainwashing, to save souls from hell.

The unbounded model doesn't much care about evangelism. If there are many ways up the mountain, or many homes on the grand estate, choosing a particular one isn't a burning concern.

The centered model witnesses to the power and joy offered by its particular center. It shares Jesus. If Karla's mom came to me and wanted to know why I'm Christian, I'd tell her. I'd unashamedly tell her that organizing my life around Jesus has given me a deeply satisfying house of being.

If her next (unlikely) question were, "Can I join you?" I'd say, "Of course! Welcome!" But if she said, "Though I respect your approach, mine's different," I wouldn't pound her over the head with her responsibility to turn Christian.

And if she said, "I can hardly bear to talk to you, your people murdered mine," I'd have to acknowledge my complicity in such sin.

If, as I believe, it's true that none of us can finally prove the rightness of *our* way, then our job is clear. It's simply to share, passionately but humbly, the meaning for us of our center, our Jesus. If this proves compelling to our partners in dialogue, we can happily welcome them into our way. If it doesn't, we let up to God the final arbitration of whose way is right.

As one who advocates taking the world into the Bible, I should examine whether any of this is remotely compatible with the Bible. I think it is. The Bible may not specifically affirm the centered model, but it does not rule out the validity of such an approach.

Wesley Ariarajah has devoted an entire book to showing this. He accepts, on the one hand, that "the

Bible stands on one firm foundation: there is one God, no other." One the other hand, he highlights examples of ways this one God breaches boundaries we might expect God to respect.

The book of Jonah affirms the one true God but depicts a "God of mercy and love who would rather forgive than destroy" even the foreigners Jonah would like destroyed. Cornelius (Acts 10) is a non-Christian with whom God speaks *before* he becomes Christian.[21]

I might add the intriguing instance of Jesus' people nearly pushing him over a cliff after he tells them God cares for such foreigners as the widow of Zarephath and Naaman the Syrian.[22] And Paul says some fascinating things about the Athenians and their unknown gods. Paul clearly affirms the centrality of the Christian way. He also takes pains to relate it to Athenian understandings.[23]

Willard G. Oxtoby identifies ways in which the Hebrews and Jesus embody a paradoxical approach to evangelism. To oversimplify a bit, he suggests that the Old Testament portrays a Hebrew people whose task is to focus on their own faithfulness to God. What goes on in the other nations is more their and God's than the Hebrews' business. The Hebrews are to let their light shine. This light can be a light to the nations, but what the nations do with it isn't the Hebrews' primary concern.[24]

Turning to Jesus, Oxtoby notes that on the one hand the New Testament clearly does portray a Jesus who is *the* way. On the other hand, "the figure of Jesus also sets aside communal boundaries and exclusive notions of truth." The Jesus who is the way tells the story of the good Samaritan, which makes the outcast, the one outside the way, the hero.[25]

There is much that one could argue here. But the centered approach to evangelism at least holds tightly to both ends of the typical arguments. It refuses to relinquish Jesus. It also refuses to make Jesus' way an excuse for coercing, brainwashing, or even killing.

I hope that together, as we each keep growing, Kristy and I can figure all this stuff out.

QUESTIONS FOR DISCUSSION AND REFLECTION

1. Which is more important? Faithfulness to particular values regardless of divisions this may cause? Or unity at the possible expense of particular commitments? Why?

2. What important contexts have shaped you? How have they shaped you?

3. How much do you think personal experience shapes our values and theologies?

4. Can we know any truth not shaped by our personal and social backgrounds?

5. Pick an issue. Divorce, alcohol, whatever. What *principle(s)* do you affirm in relation to that issue? What different *expressions* do you imagine that principle might have in different contexts? For example, suppose all agree alcohol abuse is wrong. Might there be a difference in how that principle is expressed in an urban, complex, auto-filled context versus Jesus' simpler, more agrarian one?

6. Do you find the centered model's commitment to uphold common core principles while allowing diverse expression helpful to you? Why or why not?

7. How would you answer a child's questions about the difference between his or her faith and a friend's religion?

8. Is Christianity the one true religion?

9. Is there truth in other religions?

10. Do you agree with the centered model's commitment both to affirm the centrality of Christianity truth and remain open to learning from other truths?

EPILOGUE

Trackless Wastes, Stars to Steer By, and a Home for Homesick Souls

We've traveled together as far across the trackless wastes as I know how to go. What have we learned about trackless wastes, stars to steer by, and the home for which we yearn—we homesick, homeless souls? More appropriately, perhaps (given my contextual, standpoint-dependent perspective), what have *I* learned?

Several things. First, I've learned about the stars. I've learned my stars to steer by are, in the end, that venerable and majestic Christian faith. They do indeed provide reliable guidance across the trackless wastes. From my perspective, at least, the faith has met all the exiling forces and found a way through them all.

I've learned about the trackless wastes, as well, though there have been surprises. As I began to write, I imaged the wastes as precisely that—wastes. They represented this liminal contemporary era I hoped we'd cross quickly on our way to the better era on the other side. Now I think that image is both right and wrong. It's right in that the contemporary era *is* a frightening wasteland. Millions of us do wander across it, lost in an orgy of individualism, narcissism, affluence, drugs, promiscuous sex, and misguided searches for meaning.

It's wrong in that the wasteland remains waste only as long as no guidance is offered. When guidance comes, those factors which once destroyed can become resources for creating beauty. This is what I learned as I maneuvered my way through psychology, for example. Psychology, when aimless, can help create a society of navel-gazing, self-fulfilling hedonists. When guided by Christian stars, however, it can help people become free, healthy, differentiated, ever-growing adults.

What I've learned about the home across the trackless wastes relates to this. I'm not so sure anymore that the home is *across* the wastes, out there, somewhere beyond here. I'm thinking instead that where the starlight strikes the earth, there the shimmering outlines of an evanescent but real house emerge.

I started out looking for a solid home, a home as sturdy as I imagined the old home to have been. Now, having probed deeper into things, I doubt the home I imagined is to be found or ever quite existed. There was never just one sacred canopy, one sacred home that enclosed all earth. People were often less aware than we moderns are of how many homes surrounded them, but many homes there always were.

And some eras probably saw nearly as much pluralism as ours. As I've pondered modern pluralism, I've become more aware that the early Christian era experienced its own radical pluralism.[1] Countless Greek, Roman, Persian, and Egyptian religions and cults vied for attention. Into this setting came the star of Bethlehem, offering those who would follow a star by which to steer across the trackless wastes of that day. Then, as now, you couldn't prove the way that star pointed was *the* only right way. You could only follow and see if you liked where it got you.

Where it got you was always hard to figure out. Where were you when lions mauled you and emperors burned you? Was this a proper home, this place which enmeshed you in scorn, persecution, and death? Yet even within this literal wasteland the stars of the faith touched earth. They created for you a hint of a home barely seen yet so real you were ready to die to stay in it.

That's what I'm trying to get at when I say I'm not so sure, after all, there *is* a solid home across the wastes. I was vaguely imagining a time after this liminal one in which a revitalized Christendom emerged. It would turn whole cultures into supporters of a Christian house of being. Now I'm thinking this is unlikely. It's probably not even desirable, since it would have to be forced on the many unwilling to freely choose Christianity—violating Jesus' invitation to freely and willfully carry his cross.

A better image is to see ourselves as building a shimmering, ethereal house grounded in wasteland but rising toward the stars in whose light it gleams. We won't always be quite sure the house is there. Starlight is faint and hard to see by. But if we persist, some very dark, very black, very clear nights will come. And the stars in such nights will burn strong and true. And we'll see the house glimmering, even as dawn approaches and dims it once more.

The house will be simultaneously evanescent *and* utterly reliable. It will be both hard to find in this life *and* made of walls that rise past this life, up through death and life beyond, keeping us safe even as we gasp our last earthly breath.

Meanwhile, across the plain, the houses of other ways and religions sometimes flicker. What about them? Will our house spread to include theirs? Will each house someday become a home on one great estate? Only God knows. I don't. What I know is that my house, hard to see though it sometimes is, is warm and cozy and satisfying. When I meet others who don't feel that way about their house, or who have no home at all, I'll open the door to mine and welcome them in. If they want to enter, wonderful. If they don't, I'll let God address what that means. I'll share the beauty of my stars with them. Then I'll allow the Creator of the stars decide whether to prompt those who follow other stars to follow, instead, the Christian ones.

One reason I'm so committed to my particular house is that it offers more energy than any other version I've tried. I once lived (as I've said before) in the old house my church tried to maintain. Its tenants used up a lot of energy trying to separate themselves entirely from the wasteland. If you see what's out there as ice and snow and Arctic wind, you waste most of your resources putting in insulation and burning the furnace on high.

When sickness afflicts your psyche, for instance, you close the door tighter and try a home remedy. Too many dirty thoughts, maybe. More prayer needed. Meanwhile, outside, waits a therapist who could help heal the cause of the trouble. She could help you integrate your shadow instead of repressing the dirt and making things worse, empowering the shadow to scourge you with still dirtier thoughts.

When I left that home I felt a rush of new energy. There was so much warmth out there. There were green meadows and Alpine forests and breezes blowing sweet, not just bitter cold. But then, when I found that the outside world also had its problems, that winter did sometimes come, I wasted energy trying to pretend *this* wasn't so. When I heard Christians talk about ways following Jesus gave their lives peace, purpose, and joy, I had to expend energy explaining it away, rather than letting it enrich me, move me, fill me with my own peace and joy.

Then I came to that crucial turning point where I'd traveled as far from stars to steer by as I want to go. Absent the stars, life truly did turn wasteland. I crept ever closer to thoroughly amoral, rudderless, relativistic living. Finally things got bad enough that I thought, "I need more guidance than this."

I opened myself again to the stars. For a time, as people who swing between extremes often do, I came close to total retreat. I was briefly tempted to reject forever the outside world, to give myself back to that old separation and leave the world to the devil. I didn't like the pain caused by holding extremes together.

Even while writing I've felt torn sometimes, wanting to risk all for separation one day, and all for translation the next. I feel the rift in my wavering treatment of the larger world—one moment wasteland, the next moment lovely.

I believe in my vision. I'm doing my best to live it, but it's no easy thing, especially for those of us born on the boundary between eras, longing for and fearing the old, longing for and fearing the new. No, it's not easy, but I hold tight, for dear life, to the two poles of my life.

And little by little I *am* becoming bicultural, I believe. I'm learning to live simultaneously in the secular world (which is God's) and God's heavenly realm. Many days now I truly do have energy. I can absorb strength and guidance from both the stars and the world, defending against neither, letting both enrich me.

Life is becoming a guided adventure. Adventure because there are always new things to learn, new insights to gain, new doors to open, new rooms to explore. Guided because I don't just explore at random but according to the light of God's stars.

In this guided adventure, we all can move toward and help create a bicultural Christian home which both encompasses the universe and gives shape to an often chaotic universe.

Our congregations can help us embark on such a fantastic voyage, though they needn't all focus on the same part. Our separatist congregations can celebrate the light from the stars. They can insist on the importance of the stars, of the faith. They can build telescopes to see the stars better, maybe by living, breathing, eating, and yes, even memorizing the Bible, as all good Christians once did.

Our translationist congregations can sing their praises of God's good world. They can immerse themselves in psychology and sociology and all the other "ologies." They can stir us to see the world's treasures and to remember that whenever we find wonder, God is near.

And then we can all talk to each other, star-gazers and wilderness-rovers alike, and help each other appreciate the importance of both stars to guide us and wilderness to explore. Gradually, maybe, we can weave it all together so the home we build is big enough for us all.

I hope it becomes home for people whose faith is simple faith, who sing old gospel songs, who doubt the value of newfangled ideas.

I hope it becomes home for those urban sophisticates, those professors, critics, and doubters who grin at the trite theology of the old songs.

I hope the simple folk learn gradually to trust the learned folk—and the learned folk confess that a simple gospel song sometimes says what no amount of learning can convey. Jesus loves me. Jesus is all the world to me. Take my hand, precious Lord. Guide me o'er life's stormy waves, until the lower lights burn on the shore, and I reach safe harbor in that land where stars there will be in my crown. Walk with me in the garden here, through toils and snares, so I'll know you there, when you who love sparrows and even me walk through the garden, heaven's sweet garden, to hold me forever close. Then I'll sing because I'm happy. I'll sing because I'm free, safe evermore in your arms everlasting.

I hope most deeply for a loving blend of congregations where the critics can question and Jesus can love not only for theological reasons but for those personal reasons that do underlie all theology. This is not just a theoretical thing for me, this yearning to see the gulf between diverse kinds of congregations healed. They are members of my family, these people in their different congregations. To hope people will love each other across their differences isn't only to engage in predictable pious wishing that people would get along. It's to yearn for my own family to mend.

My once-wounded relationship with my parents *is* healing, and that's a source of the energy that produced this book. But out there breathe also real people, loved people, people whose blood courses through mine, flesh of my flesh, bone of my bones. They haunt my dreams, these people. Their legacies, known and unknown, are what I live out.

Their faces I need to leave shadowed. Their names I need to keep hidden. They dwell in lands whose locations I need to keep vague. But truly they do exist, these my people, my ancestors and kin, my uncles and aunts and cousins and second cousins and cousins once removed. And there is division between us. Some of us hew to the old ways. Some to the new. We gaze in awe across the gulf made by our different choices, wondering how we could be so close and yet so distant. We're family, that's clear. But do we all belong to God's family? Of that we're not so sure.

Oh, but I have a dream (to echo that great Afro-American dreamer). I have a dream of a home big enough for those in my family (and they are there; I could name them; I could tell you their stories and why I love them) who still wear plain dresses and coats, who drive cars with black bumpers, who emigrate to places where they can be left alone to practice their pure faith.

I have a dream of a home big enough for those in my family (and they too are there; they too I could name; their stories and why I love them I also could tell you) who are divorced, who are gay and lesbian, doubt God exists, have killed themselves.

I dream of us groping from the separate sides of our perspectives toward a home, and building, each of us, a wall. We find one day that the walls are done, the home is complete (at least the part of it we can finish before we leave earth). We enter the home. We're shocked. We each thought we were building a different home, a home that had nothing to do with the others. But lo, unknown to any of us, we were building the very same home!

We pause. We stop. We stare at each other. Our bodies twitch, as they tempt us to move toward the others and throw them out. But the air in the home is warm, because there are walls to keep out the fiercest winds. And the air is fresh and sweet, because there are windows to let the smells of spring and honeysuckle waft in. We begin to cry, because the home is so special, and we want so much to be in it. Our tears soften us, and we move toward each other. We sense Jesus somewhere in the room, and a Holy Spirit trembles somewhere in our midst. We cross our great divides to weep together.

We cross our great divides, not only my family but all families, all congregations, all denominations, all people, wounded and divided and torn as we are. We cross our chasms and weep together for joy.

We live, yes, in a liminal age. But maybe the new home stands ready to rise already among us, awaiting only a big enough dream. Maybe we needn't wait for some far-off time. Maybe we need only take the unlimited construction materials God offers us and begin to build.

As the walls rise, the starlight will come down to meet them, and a home blending earth and starlight will shimmer in the night. The light will shine in the darkness, and the darkness will not overcome it.

QUESTIONS FOR DISCUSSION AND REFLECTION

1. What stars do you steer by?
2. What trackless wastes do you encounter?
3. Are there other images which capture for you the meaning of being a Christian in our age?
4. Do you agree with Frederick Büchner, who says that "most theology . . . is essentially autobiography"? Why or why not?
5. If you do agree, how is your theology autobiography? In what ways has your life story shaped your understanding of faith?
6. How is your congregation's story autobiography? What mix of people and events and relationships has created your particular congregation?
7. Are there wounds or rifts in your life story?
8. What kind of relationship do or did you have with your parents or other important family members? How has this affected your faith?
9. Are there people outside the home which is your faith? If so, do you want them in your home?
10. What is the meaning of your life? (This is a serious question.)

Notes

Introduction
1. Robert Detweiler, "Is Faith a Plot?" Lecture presented at Goshen College, Goshen, Ind., October 1987.

Chapter 1
1. Christopher Lasch, *The Culture of Narcissism: American Life in an Age of Diminishing Expectations* (New York: W. W. Norton and Co., Inc., 1979), p. 3.
2. Marlene Kropf, "We're Headed for a Crisis," *Gospel Herald*, March 8, 1988, pp. 161-163.
3. Beulah S. Hostetler, *American Mennonites and Protestant Movements: A Community Paradigm* (Scottdale, Pa.: Herald Press, 1987), pp. 245ff.
4. E. M. Wardle, "To Obey or Disobey?" *The Sword and Trumpet*, July 1988, p. 21.
5. Hostetler, p. 329.
6. Michael A. King, "Who Are You, My Audience?" *Gospel Herald*, July 28, 1987, p. 543.
7. Peter L. Berger, *The Sacred Canopy: Elements of a Sociological Theory of Religion* (New York: Doubleday and Co., 1967), p. 107.
8. William H. Willimon, "Making Christians in a Secular World," *Christian Century*, October 22, 1986, p. 914.
9. Charles S. McCoy, *When Gods Change: Hope for Theology* (Nashville: Abingdon Press, 1980), p. 48.
10. Benjamin R. Mariante, *Pluralistic Society, Pluralistic Church* (Washington: University Press of America, 1981), pp. 30-31.
11. Robert N. Bellah, Richard Madsen, William M. Sullivan, Ann Swidler, Steven M. Tipton, *Habits of the Heart: Individualism and Commitment in American Life* (New York: Harper and Row; Perennial Library, 1985), pp. 220-221.
12. Ibid., pp. 142-143.
13. James Barr, *Fundamentalism* (Philadelphia: The Westminster Press, 1977), p.24.
14. John A. T. Robinson, *Honest to God* (SCM Press Ltd., 1963; Philadelphia: Westminster Press, 1963), pp. 15-18.
15. David Martin, *A General Theory of Secularization* (New York: Harper and Row, 1978), pp. 280, 297.

Chapter 2
1. Hans Küng, *Theology for the Third Millennium: An Ecumenical View*, trans. Peter Heinegg (New York: Doubleday, 1988), pp. 131-132. Küng's book elaborates the theological implications of Thomas S. Kuhn's work on paradigms and their role in the development of science in *The Structure of Scientific Revolutions*. Though our ideas diverge at points, Küng's belief that ours is a time of theological "paradigm change" parallels my own sense that we're in a liminal era in which old paradigms don't satisfy and new ones are still in their infancy.
2. Ibid.

3. Jack B. Rogers and Donald K. McKim, *The Authority and Interpretation of the Bible: An Historical Approach* (San Francisco: Harper and Row, 1979), p. 235.

4. Ibid., pp. 457ff.

5. Paul E. Little, *Know Why You Believe* (Wheaton: Victor Books, 1967), p. 53.

6. Mark A. Noll, *Between Faith and Criticism: Evangelicals, Scholarship and the Bible in America* (San Francisco: Harper and Row, 1986), p. 145.

7. Ibid., p. 151.

8. Robert Grant with David Tracy, *A Short History of the Interpretation of the Bible*, 2d ed. (Philadelphia: Fortress Press, 1984), p. 93.

9. Robert Gnuse, *The Authority of the Bible: Theories of Inspiration, Revelation and the Canon of Scripture* (New York: Paulist Press, 1985), pp. 46-47.

10. Ibid., pp. 66-67.

11. Grant with Tracy, pp. 134-135.

12. Ibid., p. 129.

13. Harold S. Bender, *The Anabaptist Vision* (Scottdale, Pa.: Herald Press, 1944).

14. Leonard Gross, foreword to *Becoming Anabaptist: The Origin and Significance of Sixteenth-Century Anabaptism*, by J. Denny Weaver (Scottdale, Pa.: Herald Press, 1987), p. 10.

15. My rather free interpretation and simplification of his ideas comes from Paul Ricoeur, "The Hermeneutics of Symbols and Philosophical Reflection," in *The Philosophy of Paul Ricoeur: An Anthology of His Work*, ed. Charles E. Reagan and David Stewart (Boston: Beacon Press, 1978), pp. 36-60.

16. John R. W. Stott, "Are Evangelicals Fundamentalists?" *Christianity Today*, September 8, 1978, p. 46, quoted in Rogers and McKim.

17. Noll, p. 165.

18. Grant, p. 129.

19. The Interpreter's Dictionary of the Bible, s.v. (Nashville: Abingdon), "Science and the Bible," by W. G. Pollard, p. 790.

20. Madeleine L'Engle, *Walking on Water: Reflections on Faith and Art* (Wheaton: Harold Shaw, 1980), pp. 55, 86.

21. Michael A. King, "Prowlers, Prayers and Dream," *Christian Century*, November 4, 1987, pp. 959-960.

22. C. Norman Kraus, *Jesus Christ Our Lord: Christology from a Disciple's Perspective* (Scottdale, Pa.: Herald Press, 1987).

23. George R. Brunk II, *A Trumpet Sound: A Crisis Among Mennonites on the Doctrine of Christ* (Harrisonburg, Va.: Heralds of Hope, Inc., 1988).

Chapter 3

1. Peter L. Berger, *The Sacred Canopy: Elements of a Sociological Theory of Religion* (New York: Doubleday and Co., 1967), p. 149.

2. Lesslie Newbigin, *Foolishness to the Greeks: The Gospel and Western Culture* (Grand Rapids: William B. Eerdmans, 1986), p. 54.

3. Glenda Hope, "Revisioning Seminary as Ministry-Centered," *Christian Century*, February 1-8, 1989, p. 107.

4. Mark I. Wallace, "The New Yale Theology," *Christian Scholars Review* XVII:2 (December 1987): pp. 154-155.

5. George A. Lindbeck, *The Nature of Doctrine: Religion and Theology in a Postliberal Age* (Philadelphia: Westminster Press, 1984), pp. 16-27.

6. Ibid., p. 22.

7. Ibid.
8. Ibid., p. 34.
9. Ibid., p. 118
10. Neill Q. Hamilton, *Maturing in the Christian Life: A Pastor's Guide* (Philadelphia: Geneva Press, 1984).
11. Charles V. Gerkin, *Widening the Horizons: Pastoral Responses to a Fragmented Society* (Philadelphia: Westminster Press, 1986), p. 130.
12. June Alliman Yoder quoted in Kathy Nofziger, "June Alliman Yoder: Teacher, Preacher, Student," *Gospel Herald*, January 31, 1989, p. 69.
13. Stanley Hauerwas, *The Peaceable Kingdom: A Primer in Christian Ethics* (Notre Dame: University of Notre Dame Press, 1983), pp. 24-25.
14. For a fuller treatment of reversal, see Ronald J. Sider and Michael A. King, *Preaching About Life in a Threatening World* (Philadelphia: Westminster Press, 1987) pp. 53-60.
15. William H. Willimon and Robert L. Wilson, *Rekindling the Flame: Strategies for a Vital United Methodism* (Nashville: Abingdon Press, 1987), pp. 27-29.
16. Ibid., p. 29.
17. Stanley Hauerwas, *A Community of Character: Toward a Constructive Christian Social Ethic* (Notre Dame: University of Notre Dame Press, 1981), p. 50.
18. Ibid., p. 51.
19. Os Guinness, *The Gravedigger File: Papers on the Subversion of the Modern Church* (Downers Grove, Ill: InterVarsity Press, 1983), pp. 220-221.

Chapter 4
1. Arthur F. Holmes, *Contours of a World View* (Grand Rapids: William B. Eerdmans Publishing Co., 1983), p. 50.
2. Ibid., p. 53.
3. Josh. 7:1, 18-20, 24; 22:20.
4. George A. Lindbeck, *The Nature of Doctrine: Religion and Theology in a Postliberal Age* (Philadelphia: Westminster Press, 1984), p. 21.
5. Charles V. Gerkin, *Widening the Horizons: Pastoral Responses to a Fragmented Society* (Philadelphia: Westminster Press, 1984), p. 14.
6. Abraham H. Maslow, *Motivation and Personality* (New York: Harper and Row, 1954), quoted in Frank G. Goble, *The Third Force: The Psychology of Abraham Maslow* (New York: Pocket Books, 1970), p. 24.
7. John A. Sanford, *Evil: The Shadow Side of Reality* (New York: Crossroad, 1988), p. 49.
8. Ibid., pp. 58-59.
9. Donald Capps, "Religion and Psychological Well-Being," in *The Sacred in a Secular Age: Toward Revision in the Scientific Study of Religion*, ed. Phillip E. Hammond (Berkeley: University of California Press, 1985), pp. 241-242.
10. Luke 15:11-32.
11. Gen. 11-13.
12. Gen. 18:22-33.
13. Amos 5:21.
14. Matt. 12:1-8.
15. See Joseph Campbell with Bill Moyers, *The Power of Myth*, ed. Betty Sue Flowers (New York: Doubleday, 1988), p. 91.

16. Matt. 11:28-30
17. Luke 7:36-50.
18. Sanford, pp. 79-80.
19. Ibid., p. 80.
20. Ibid., pp. 71, 83.

Chapter 5
1. Paul Hiebert, "The Category 'Christian' in the Mission Task," *International Review of Missions* 272 (July 1983), pp. 421–427. Jim Derstine, of Mennonite Board of Missions, deserves credit for bringing this article to my attention.
2. Ibid., pp. 421–423.
3. Charles V. Gerkin, *Widening the Horizons: Pastoral Responses to a Fragmented Society* (Philadelphia: Westminster Press, 1986), p. 33. Gerkin derives his family typology from David Kantor and William Lehr, *Inside the Family* (San Francisco: Jossey-Bass, 1975).
4. Robert Jewett, *Christian Tolerance: Paul's Message to the Modern Church* (Philadelphia: Westminster Press, 1982), pp. 68-91.
5. Ibid., p. 85. Jewett avoids blatant anti-Semitism in discussing Paul's critique of the Jews, but in an instance like this it's important to remember Paul was a Jew critiquing other Jews. As an insider, he had the right to do this. We outsiders need to be careful not to fall into a Christian freedom/Jewish legalism dichotomy which easily leads to anti-Semitism. Perhaps it's most helpful to see Paul as identifying a tendency to which all people—not only Jews—can yield.
6. Hiebert, pp. 424-425.
7. Gerkin, p. 33.
8. Jewett, p. 71.
9. Ibid., pp. 73-77.
10. Hiebert, p. 423.
11. Gerkin, p. 33.
12. Jewett, pp. 36-37.
13. Robert C. Worley, *A Gathering of Strangers: Understanding the Life of Your Church* (Philadelphia: Westminster Press, 1983), p. 94.
14. Ibid., pp. 95-97.
15. Examples of faith development thinking include James W. Fowler, Robin W. Lovin, and others, *Trajectories in Faith: Five Life Stories* (Nashville: Abingdon, 1980), and Neill Q. Hamilton, *Maturing in the Christian Life: A Pastor's Guide* (Philadelphia: Geneva Press, 1984).

Chapter 6
1. J. Denny Weaver, *Becoming Anabaptist: The Origin and Significance of Sixteenth-Century Anabaptism* (Scottdale, Pa.: Herald Press, 1987), pp. 129-141.
2. C. René Padilla, *Mission Between the Times: Essays on the Kingdom* (Grand Rapids: William B. Eerdmans Co., 1985), pp. 105-106.
3. Michael A. King, "Where Would Jesus Meet Sinners Today?" *Gospel Herald*, March 24, 1987, pp. 194-195. "The Night Jesus Danced at the Saddleboot Bar," a different article making a similar point, has also been accepted for publication by *Christian Century*.

4. Letty M. Russell, *Household of Freedom: Authority in Feminist Theology* (Philadelphia: Westminster Press, 1987), pp. 30-31.

5. Ibid.

6. Alan Race, *Christians and Religious Pluralism: Patterns in the Christian Theology of Religions* (Maryknoll: Orbis Books, 1982), p. 10.

7. Ted Peters, "A Theology of Interreligious Dialogue," *Christian Century*, October 15, 1986, p. 883.

8. Harvey Cox, *Many Mansions: A Christian's Encounter with Other Faiths* (Boston: Beacon Press, 1988), p. 10.

9. Ibid., p. 18.

10. Race, pp. 38-47.

11. Peters, pp. 883-884.

12. Cox, p. 10.

13. Hans Küng, *Theology for the Third Millennium: An Ecumenical View*, trans. Peter Heinegg (New York: Doubleday, 1988), pp. 230-235.

14. Cox, pp. 18.

15. Peters, p. 884.

16. Lesslie Newbigin, *The Open Secret: Sketches for a Missionary Theology* (Grand Rapids: William B. Eerdmans Co., 1978), p. 190.

17. Cox, pp. 14-15.

18. Küng, pp. 248-253, comments helpfully on the distinction between internal and external perspectives on Christianity.

19. Cox, pp. 2-3.

20. William H. Willimon, "Truth and the Postliberal Church," *Christian Century*, January 28, 1987, p. 83.

21. S. Wesley Ariarajah, *The Bible and People of Other Faiths* (Geneva: World Council of Churches, 1985), pp. 1, 13-18.

22. Luke 4:24-30.

23. Acts 17:22-32.

24. Willard G. Oxtoby, *The Meaning of Other Faiths* (Philadelphia: Westminster Press, 1983), pp. 17-23.

25. Ibid., pp. 30-31.

Epilogue

1. C. Norman Kraus deserves credit for pointing this out to me.

Bibliography

Ariarajah, S. W.
   1985 *The Bible and People of Other Faiths*. Geneva: World Council of Churches.

Barr, J.
   1977 *Fundamentalism*. Philadelphia: Westminster Press.

Bellah, R. N.; Richard Madsen; W. M. Sullivan; A. Swidler; S. M. Tipton
   1985 *Habits of the Heart: Individualism and Commitment in American Life*. New York: Harper and Row; Perennial Library.

Bender, H. S.
   1944 *The Anabaptist Vision*. Scottdale, Pa.: Herald Press.

Berger, P.
   1967 *The Sacred Canopy: Elements of a Sociological Theory of Religion*. New York: Doubleday and Co.
   1973 *The Homeless Mind: Modernization and Consciousness*. New York: Random House.
   1977 *Facing Up to Modernity: Excursions in Sociology, Politics and Religion*. New York: Basic Books.
   1979 *The Heretical Imperative: The Continuing Possibility of Religious Affirmation*. Anchor Press, 1979.

Brunk II, G. R.
   1988 *A Trumpet Sound: A Crisis Among Mennonites*

on the Doctrine of Christ. Harrisonburg, Va.: Heralds of Hope, Inc.

Campbell, J., with B. Moyers
1988 *The Power of Myth*. Ed. Betty Sue Flowers. New York: Doubleday.

Capps, D.
1985 "Religion and Psychological Well-Being." In *The Sacred in a Secular Age: Toward Revision in the Scientific Study of Religion*. Ed. Phillip E. Hammond. Berkeley: University of California Press.

Cox, H.
1988 *Many Mansions: A Christian's Encounter with Other Faiths*. Boston: Beacon Press.

Fenn, R.
1978 *Toward a Theory of Secularization*. Storrs, Conn.: Society for the Scientific Study of Religion.

Fowler, J. W.; Robin W. Lovin; and others
1980 *Trajectories in Faith: Five Life Stories*. Nashville: Abingdon.

Gerkin, C. V.
1986 *Widening the Horizons: Pastoral Responses to a Fragmented Society*. Philadelphia: Westminster Press.

Gnuse, R.
1985 *The Authority of the Bible: Theories of Inspiration, Revelation and the Canon of Scripture*. New York: Paulist Press.

Grant, R., with D. Tracy
1984 *A Short History of the Interpretation of the Bible*, sec. ed. Philadelphia: Fortress.

Gross, L.
    1987   Foreword to *Becoming Anabaptist: The Origin and Significance of Sixteenth-Century Anabaptism*, by J. Denny Weaver. Scottdale: Herald Press.

Guinness, O.
    1983   *The Gravedigger File: Papers on the Subversion of the Modern Church.* Downers Grove, Ill.: InterVarsity.

Hamilton, N. Q.
    1984   *Maturing in the Christian Life: A Pastor's Guide.* Philadelphia: Geneva Press.

Hauerwas, S.
    1981   *A Community of Character: Toward a Constructive Christian Social Ethic.* Notre Dame: University of Notre Dame Press.
    1983   *The Peaceable Kingdom: A Primer in Christian Ethics.* Notre Dame: University of Notre Dame Press.

Hiebert, P.
    1983   "The Category 'Christian' in the Mission Task." *International Review of Missions.* 272:421-427.

Holmes, A. F.
    1983   *Contours of a World View.* Grand Rapids: William B. Eerdmans Publishing Co.

Hope, G.
    1989   "Revisioning Seminary as Ministry-Centered." *Christian Century.* February 1-8:107-111.

Hopewell, J. F.
    1987   *Congregation: Stories and Structures.* Ed. Barbara G. Wheeler. Philadelphia: Fortress Press.

Hostetler, B. S.
   1987 *American Mennonites and Protestant Movements: A Community Paradigm*. Scottdale, Pa.: Herald Press.

Jewett, R.
   1982 *Christian Tolerance: Paul's Message to the Modern Church*. Philadelphia: Westminster Press.

Kraus, C. N.
   1987 *Jesus Christ Our Lord: Christology from a Disciple's Perspective*. Scottdale, Pa.: Herald Press.

Küng, H.
   1988 *Theology for the Third Millennium: An Ecumenical View*. Trans. Peter Heinegg. New York: Doubleday and Co.

L'Engle, M.
   1980 *Walking on Water: Reflections on Faith and Art*. Wheaton: Harold Shaw.

Lasch, C.
   1979 *The Culture of Narcissism: American Life in an Age of Diminishing Expectations*. New York: W. W. Norton and Co., Inc.

Lindbeck, G. A.
   1984 *The Nature of Doctrine: Religion and Theology in a Postliberal Age*. Philadelphia: Westminster Press.

Little, P. E.
   1967 *Know Why You Believe*. Wheaton: Victor Books.

Manschreck, C. L., ed.
   1971 *Erosion of Authority*. Nashville: Abingdon Press.

Mariante, B. R.
    1981   *Pluralistic Society, Pluralistic Church.* Washington: University Press of America.

Martin, D.
    1978   *A General Theory of Secularization.* New York: Harper and Row.

Marty, M. E.
    1989   "The Years of the Evangelicals." *Christian Century.* Feb. 15:171-174.

Maslow, A. H.
    1954   *Motivation and Personality.* New York: Harper and Row. Quoted in Goble, F. G. *The Third Force: The Psychology of Abraham Maslow.* New York: Pocket Books, 1970.

McCoy, C. S.
    1980   *When Gods Change: Hope for Theology.* Nashville: Abingdon Press.

Newbigin, L.
    1966   *Honest Religion for Secular Man.* Westminster Press.
    1978   *The Open Secret: Sketches for a Missionary Theology.* Grand Rapids: William B. Eerdmans Co.
    1986   *Foolishness to the Greeks: The Gospel and Western Culture.* Grand Rapids: William B. Eerdmans Co.

Nofziger, K.
    1989   "June Alliman Yoder: Teacher, Preacher, Student." *Gospel Herald.* January 31:68-69.

Noll, M. A.
  1986 *Between Faith and Criticism: Evangelicals, Scholarship and the Bible in America.* San Francisco: Harper and Row.

Oxtoby, W. G.
  1983 *The Meaning of Other Faiths.* Philadelphia: Westminster Press.

Padilla, R.
  1985 *Mission Between the Times: Essays on the Kingdom.* Grand Rapids: William B. Eerdmans Co.

Peters, T.
  1986 "A Theology of Interreligious Dialogue." *Christian Century.* October 15:883-885.

Race, A.
  1982 *Christians and Religious Pluralism: Patterns in the Christian Theology of Religions.* Maryknoll: Orbis Books.

Ricoeur, P.
  1978 "The Hermeneutics of Symbols and Philosophical Reflection." In *The Philosophy of Paul Ricoeur: An Anthology of His Work.* Ed. Charles E. Reagan and David Stewart. Boston: Beacon Press.

Robinson, J. A. T.
  1963 *Honest to God.* Philadelphia: Westminster Press.

Rogers, J. B., and D. K. McKim
  1979 *The Authority and Interpretation of the Bible: An Historical Approach.* San Francisco: Harper and Row.

Russell, L. M.
　1987　*Household of Freedom: Authority in Feminist Theology*. Philadelphia: Westminster Press.

Sanford, J. A.
　1988　*Evil: The Shadow Side of Reality*. New York: Crossroad.

Sider, R. J., and M. A. King
　1987　*Preaching About Life in a Threatening World*. Philadelphia: Westminster Press.

Wallace, M. I.
　1987　"The New Yale Theology." *Christian Scholars Review* XVII:2 (Dec.) 154-170.

Willimon, William H.
　1986　"Making Christians in a Secular World." *Christian Century*. October 22:914-917.
　1987　"Truth and the Postliberal Church." *Christian Century*. January 28:82-85.

Willimon, William H., and Robert L. Wilson
　1987　*Rekindling the Flame: Strategies for a Vital United Methodism*. Nashville: Abingdon Press.

Worley, Robert C.
　1983　*A Gathering of Strangers: Understanding the Life of Your Church*. Philadelphia: Westminster Press.

Wardle, E. M.
　1988　"To Obey or Disobey?" *The Sword and Trumpet*. July:21-22.

The Author

Though he is currently book editor at Herald Press, King's book grew out of seven years (1982–1989) of pastoring at Germantown Mennonite Church, Philadelphia, Pennsylvania, the oldest Mennonite Church in North America. During much of that time, he also worked part-time in home repairs. He was pastoral intern at Diamond Street Mennonite Church, Philadelphia (1980–1982).

King has coauthored (with Ronald J. Sider) a book on social issue preaching, *Preaching About Life in a Threatening World* (Westminster, 1987). He has had over eighty articles published in a wide variety of Christian magazines and writes a monthly column for *Christian Living*. He has spoken in many church settings, including national assemblies, high schools and colleges, conferences, retreats, and local congregations.

The oldest of nine children, King was born in Sellersville, Pennsylvania, but soon taken to Cuba by his missionary parents, Aaron and Betty King. He lived in Cuba until age five, then in Mexico until age seventeen. In Mexico, during whatever time he could spare from reading countless books, he went to high school by taking correspondence courses from the University of Nebraska Extension Division.

He is married to Joan Kenerson King, of Olean, New York, a registered nurse with an M.S.N. in psychiatric nursing. They are parents of Kristy, Katie, and Rachael and share parenting and homemaking as equally as possible.

King holds an M.Div. from Eastern Baptist Theological Seminary, Philadelphia, Pennsylvania; and a B.A. in Bible and Philosophy from Eastern Mennonite College, Harrisonburg, Virginia.

King is a member of the Franconia Conference Leadership Commission and its Administrative Committee.

He attends Salford Mennonite Church, Harleysville, Pennsylvania, where he preaches once a month.